Symbols
SIGNPOSTS OF DEVOTION

(Revised)

by
Ratha Doyle McGee

•

Illustrated by
Bodo José Weber
and
Ernest A. Pickup

•

THE UPPER ROOM
The World's Most Widely Used Devotional Guide
and

Other Devotional Literature

1908 Grand Avenue • Nashville, Tennessee 37203

Dedicated to

A. B. S. ♀ and G. A. S. ⊕

whose lives and personal symbols
inspire me to seek new ways to
share Christian truths

Library of Congress Catalog Card Number: 62-21157

Sixth Printing

UR-92-60-15-0164
Printed in the United States of America

INTRODUCTION

Because of the greatly increased interest in symbolism among Protestant churches, The Upper Room presents this little book by Ratha Doyle McGee. There are not many books in the field, and there is real need for some inexpensive book which tells the story of the most used symbols.

Not only is the use of symbols as old as the Christian church but symbols were well known in Old Testament times. The Temple helped to create them, and the synagogues have kept many of the symbols alive. It is not correct to say that there has been a rediscovery of symbolism. It is better to say that there is a renewed interest in the subject. In the days of early Protestantism many churches were built without the use of any symbols; but in every generation since the days of Martin Luther, Protestant churches have been built in which symbols were used. These churches are in existence today and give evidence of the respect in which symbols were held. Because of the fear that symbols might become objects of worship, Protestants have at times been slow to use them, but outstanding old churches in many lands have kept alive the historic representations of the great signs of our Christian faith. When frequently there has been no other, the cross has been the one symbol used in the church; if not on the altar, then on a window or a door or the furniture, or on the top of the steeple.

This little book gives the main symbols with drawings of each. The drawings have been done by Bodo José Weber and Ernest A. Pickup, and the editorial work has been done chiefly by Sulon G. Ferree of The Upper Room editorial staff. The symbols are primarily useful as aids to worship though sometimes they have been used as objects of worship quite contrary to Protestant tradition. They can be most effectively used to remind the worshiper of the historical backgrounds of our Christian faith and the doctrines in which we believe. For instance, the various symbols of the Trinity, such as the triangle, fleur-de-lis, the trefoil, or the shamrock all remind one that the Godhead is three persons in one.

Here in Nashville in The Upper Room Chapel are many symbols which tie into the ideas of the Last Supper and the upper room. The chancel has twelve symbols carved in wood representing the twelve apostles, with the rayed cross representing Paul, who has been substituted for Judas. The symbols on the gate of the chancel represent the Father, Son, and Holy Spirit, and the four Evangels. Other symbols are used in the chapel, the Grover C. Emmons Prayer Room, and the Pentecost or World Christian Fellowship Window. Pictures of these are used in this book.

Thousands of people visit The Upper Room Chapel annually; and Mildred Anderson Cate, the hostess of the chapel, has prepared much of the chapel data that is used in the chapel and in this book.

Christians are becoming more and more responsive to values of worship and devotions found in the symbols. There are many ways in which this book may be used. Its widest use will be by individual church members who desire to know the meaning of the symbols in their own churches. Where new churches are being built or old churches are being remodeled, this book will help members of the congregation to be prepared for a proper reception and understanding of the symbols. Women's groups are especially interested in the study of symbols, and they need a small book like this for their use. Likewise, youth groups are eager for knowledge of symbols and their use. Youth will find this book helpful. Children's classes, especially pastors' instruction classes, will find it useful also. Because of the frequent use of symbols by various men's organizations, Masons and others, it will be appreciated by men's groups.

The index has been carefully prepared. It may be used with profit to locate the various symbols and to find their relationships to one another, especially since there are many instances of more than one symbol for the same idea.

We commend *Symbols—Signposts of Devotion* to you.

J. MANNING POTTS
Editor, *The Upper Room*
Nashville, Tennessee

CONTENTS

ILLUSTRATIONS

BIBLIOGRAPHY

Adams, W. H. Davenport. *The Catacombs of Rome.* London, Thomas Nelson and Sons.

Benson, George William. *The Cross, Its History and Symbolism.* Buffalo, Privately printed, 1934.

Breasted, James H. *Development of Religion and Thought in Ancient Egypt.* New York, Charles Scribner's Sons, 1912.

Dalton, O. M. *A Guide to the Early Christian and Byzantine Antiquities.* Oxford University Press, London, 1903.

Griffith, Helen S. *The Sign Language of Our Faith.* New York, Morehouse-Gorham Company, 1944.

Hulme, F. Edward. *The History, Principles and Practice of Symbolism in Christian Art.* New York, The Macmillan Company, 1909.

Kretzmann, Adalbert R. *Symbols, A Practical Handbook.* Chicago, The Walther League, 1944.

Lowrie, Walter. *Art in the Early Church.* New York, American Book-Stratford Press, Inc., 1947.

Lundy, John P. *Monumental Christianity.* New York, J. W. Bouton, 1876.

MacKenzie, Donald A. *The Migration of Symbols.* New York, Alfred A. Knopf, 1926.

Reifenberg, Adolf. *Ancient Hebrew Arts.* New York, The Spiral Press, 1950.

Stafford, Thomas A. *Christian Symbolism in the Evangelical Churches.* Nashville, Abingdon-Cokesbury Press, 1942.

Treeck, C. V. and Croft, Aloysius. *Symbols in the Church.* Milwaukee, The Bruce Publishing Company, 1936.

Vogt, Von Ogden. *Art and Religion.* New Haven, Yale University Press, 1929.

Webber, Fredrick Roth. *Church Symbolism.* Cleveland, J. H. Jansen, 1938.

FOREWORD AND ACKNOWLEDGMENTS

It is not possible to give a complete list of the great number of people to whom thanks and appreciation are due. However, for their kind and constant help, Drs. Rhoda C. Edmeston and Lindsey P. Pherigo of Scarritt College, Nashville, Tennessee, are due special mention. Dr. Pherigo was the director of an original research project titled "The Origin of Christian Symbols in Use Before A.D. 325." He also helped guide the organization and research of my master's thesis, *The Scriptural Justification of Our Protestant Symbols*. The thesis was completed under Dr. Edmeston's direction because Dr. Pherigo went away for further graduate study. Much of the material herein was also in the thesis.

Common use has been the single criterion for determining which symbols should be included in this study. I have tried to compare the importance which various books ascribe to particular symbols and then draw my own conclusions. A list of these books is available in the bibliography. In addition to this literary weighing, personal observations have been made of symbols displayed in many churches.

The following books have been very helpful in the preparation of this book. Thomas A. Stafford's *Christian Symbolism in the Evangelical Churches* has been especially helpful as to what symbols are appropriate for Protestant churches. Helen Stuart Griffith's *The Sign Language of Our Faith* and A. R. Kretzmann's *Symbols* have both been valuable because of their fine drawings.

No treatise on symbols would be complete without mention of F. R. Webber's *Church Symbolism*. This is a classic and can be studied profitably by anyone who remembers that the author includes both Roman Catholic and Protestant symbols without clearly pointing out the differences. Christian symbols are, in the main, the same; but some symbols are peculiarly Protestant while others belong to Roman Catholicism.

There are many kinds of symbolism even within the Church. But in order to limit the field, this book makes no effort to deal with the symbolism of color, arrangement, tone, or act.

It hopes, rather, to discuss only the symbolism of those symbols that are *commonly depicted* in Protestant churches.

In America the word *Protestant* and the word *Evangelical* have usually the same meaning, but there is still not complete agreement as to which churches fall into this group. For our purpose we will consider as Protestant those churches that use the term to define their own position.

By *depicted* we mean that they are concretely shown solely for the purpose of symbolizing an idea and are not of themselves used for any other purpose than that of conveying a message. The baptismal font, for example, is excluded because it serves as a container for the water used in baptism, in addition to being symbolic of the state which baptism produces. However, if the baptismal font commonly appeared in stained-glass windows, it would be included because there it is a symbol of the regeneration of man. The same rule is followed regarding the altar. In actual existence it is an entity, and therefore not basically a depicted symbol. However, whenever the altar appears in a conventionalized form in a drawing or a window, it symbolizes Old Testament worship or Holy Communion. Perhaps, at this point, it will be wise to explain that any symbol should be displayed in such a way as to remind the viewers not of itself, but of the idea behind it. Good symbols, like good soloists, call attention to the message, not the messenger.

The word *symbol* is used throughout these pages in its broadest sense. This means that in scope it covers the technical terms *symbol, emblem, figure,* and *type.* Helen Griffith defines a symbol as setting forth being or character; an emblem as a visible representation of an attribute, truth, or doctrine; a figure as an imaginary creation, presenting an allegory or metaphor; and a type as typifying a historical character.

James Strong's *Exhaustive Concordance of the Bible* has been used to locate pertinent scripture references. Whenever scripture has been found relating to the symbol, some reference has been given to it along with the symbol's name. Where no verse or verses of scripture are given either with the symbol's name or in the body of material, no specific scripture reference was found.

Scripture verses quoted are from the Revised Standard Version of the Holy Bible, and are used by permission of the Division of Christian Education of the National Council of the Churches of Christ in the United States of America.

The illustrations were done by Mr. Bodo Weber and Mr. Ernest A. Pickup. The lines are original, but the ideas came from the churches, books, and authors mentioned elsewhere in this foreword.

In as far as possible, the symbols are arranged chronologically within each chapter by the common names of the objects pictured. The chapters of the book, in as far as possible, are arranged chronologically also, in order to give the reader a better historical perspective of God's revelation of his Word to mankind. An alphabetical index and a symbol index are found in the back of the book.

—RATHA DOYLE McGEE

CHAPTER I

SIGNPOSTS, DETOURS, AND THE ROAD MAP

MOST of us have trouble with our daily devotions. These important periods often lack content and direction. There are at least two reasons why such difficulties beset even the earnestly seeking Christian. The first reason is our thoughts do not move readily from everyday matters to the verities of God. Our minds need trains of thought to transport them to the islands of worship; we need signposts to show us the way. The second reason is that the mill of the mind needs grist to grind. No grist, no meal—spiritual or otherwise.

If properly learned and used, the great symbols of the Christian church provide both direction and content. They are truly *Signposts of Devotion*. They point the way for our devotion to go, and they remind us of the devotion and sacrifice of those who have gone before. They give guidance and grist.

There is neither space here nor the wish to go into a discussion of the definition of meaning. However, it might be well to make this suggestion to those who would think more deeply concerning symbols. Perhaps one devotional roadblock is that, in our Christian contemplation, we attempt to do that for which our minds are not trained. We try to think of God and his attributes in a general way, whereas in almost every other thought process we go from the *specific* to the *general*. It is difficult, at least for most of us, to think of a godlike Being. Our finite minds cannot comprehend such infiniteness. However, the more we learn about Christ, the easier we find it to think of him and then of the Christlike God he reveals. This is the great contribution that Jesus Christ made to us.

We are an object-minded people. Our thoughts are expressed in terms of objects. Our communication of ideas often depends upon our ability to cause other persons to visualize specifically that which we are discussing in a general way. If communication has taken place, they may say, "I *see* what you mean." Symbols are man's means of *seeing* what is meant. For this reason, Christian symbols can be a most important aid to our devotional life. They help us to objectify ideas and yet do not limit our devotional thoughts to their particular representation.

In order to help us when we desire to know God better but do not care to think, let us consider this analogy. If we cannot read the road map or understand the signposts, we often run into a dead end or at least a detour. We must think in order to travel the road of worship. Christian symbols help us think of God. If we seek enough, surrender enough, and serve enough, then, some day, for us to think will be to worship.

The main road map for the Christian is the Bible. If anyone is to travel far, he must use it as his guide as to where to go and how to get there. He must first learn to follow the everyday road before he can mount up with wings like an eagle. Devotional flight is achieved only by those who are willing to walk awhile on the ground.

The hallowed ground we need to walk on is the Bible. All of our signposts must be examined in the light of it. For that reason, we try here to give the general attitude the Bible expresses toward symbols and then consider each symbol on its own merit.

According to the Old Testament writers, God himself taught the people by means of symbols. The flaming sword placed to guard the Garden of Eden, mentioned in Genesis 3:24, was a symbol of the authority of God. The "mark on Cain," told of in Genesis 4:15, was a symbol to be read by all men. The lamb's blood placed on the doorposts and lintels, described in Exodus 12:7, was a symbol ordained by God. The bronze serpent of Numbers 21:9 was a symbol.

These are but a few of the symbols found in the Old Testament. But some of them as well as others are used in the New Testament. Hebrews, Revelation, and John rely more heavily upon Old Testament symbolism than do the other New Testament books. But they are not alone in the use of this excellent means of communication. For example, the *crown,* which is a symbol of Christ's kingship and our reward, is spoken of as the "crown of life" in James 1:12 and in Revelation 2:10.

All four Gospels describe the descent of the Holy Spirit upon Jesus at his baptism with the words "as" or "like a dove." Is it any wonder that a dove is the most widely known symbol of the Holy Spirit?

Christian symbols in their relationship to the Bible fall into one of three groups. I. The first group, Group I, is composed of those symbols that were used as symbols or as metaphors in the Bible. One example of this group is the *rainbow.* II. The second section, Group II, has symbols that came into common use early in the life of the Church because of an incident or occurrence recorded in the Bible. A particular object described in the account, by its relation to the story, has come to symbolize the event itself. Some examples of this group are the *dove,* the *chalice,* the *cross.* III. The third group, Group III, contains symbols that are inventions or applications of things not mentioned in the Bible but are nevertheless thought to be adequate to express biblical ideas. Examples are the *circle,* the *triangle,* and the *phoenix.*

Any person who takes the Bible as the standard of his or her Christianity will not deny the Church the use of such symbols as the rainbow. In Genesis 9:13 God says, "I set my bow in the cloud, and it shall be a sign of the covenant between me and the earth." It seems that God, at least in the eyes of the author of this portion of scripture, is ordaining the use of this symbol and approving the use of symbols in general. If we hold that any symbol employed within the pages of the Bible is helpful when used in a Christian society, we are approving the use of symbols. The authors of the Bible used symbols widely. If we give assent to the use of those which they used, is it not just as sensible to employ others to express the ideas which they believed to be important? The idea is more important than the method of presentation. An intelligent use of symbolism is a helpful means of getting across to the heart and mind of man the truths of God as revealed in Christ Jesus.

CHAPTER II

SYMBOLS FROM THE OLD TESTAMENT

God Spoke of Old

"I N many and various ways God spoke of old to our fathers by the prophets." So says the first verse of the book of Hebrews. Part of the message that these prophets gave to the people is to be found in the Old Testament. We agree completely with the second verse of Hebrews which says, "but in these last days he has spoken to us by a Son." But we believe that much is to be gained by a study of the symbols found in the Old Testament. Indeed, almost all the New Testament ideas have their roots deep in the Old Testament. It is very doubtful if we can really understand the New Testament without knowing the Old. Thus, in this chapter it is my desire to lift up those symbols that have been important through the ages. Of course, our understanding of these symbols is enriched by our Christian tradition.

God's message has not changed; rather man's understanding has grown. God spoke of old to the prophets, and God still speaks—through his Son and through his signs.

Symbols of particular persons, although they may be from the Old Testament, are not included in this chapter. They may be found in the chapter in which those persons are discussed.

Figure 1

APPLE—Fall of Man
Genesis, Chapter 3

An *apple* is the symbol of the fall of man or of his sinful (fallen) nature. The verses in Genesis which tell of the Fall do not in any place describe the type of tree from which Eve ate fruit. Thus the very common belief that she ate an apple is an assumption which is not supported by scripture but is so widespread that almost any person retelling the story says that the fruit was an apple. Because of this widespread belief, the *apple* or a tree with an apple on it, sometimes with a snake coiled around its trunk, is the symbol of the fall of man. Technically, since scripture does not describe the fruit, this symbol falls into group III. But if one is not too literalistic, it may be included in Group II. (*See* page 13 for meanings of groups I, II, III.)

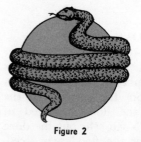

Figure 2

SNAKE
Fall of Man and Spread of Sin
Genesis 3:13

As a result of the story about the serpent tempting Eve to eat of the fruit of the tree which was in the midst of the garden, the *snake* or *serpent* has come to be the symbol of deceit and slyness, of greed and sin, and particularly of the fall of man. To the author of this story the *fall* was the result of sin in the guise of a serpent. The snake is very often shown coiled around the tree from which the fruit supposedly came. To symbolize the spread of sin throughout the whole earth, it is customary to show the earth with a snake coiled completely around it.

Since it is not used symbolically in the scriptures, this symbol falls into group III.

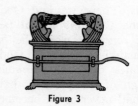

Figure 3

ARK
Old Testament Worship; Salvation
Genesis 6:14-16 Exodus 25:10-22

There are two *arks* in the scriptures: the Ark of the Covenant, which symbolizes the presence of God in the human community, and Noah's Ark. Bible references to both of these are numerous. The story of Noah's Ark begins at Genesis 6:14, and the Ark of the Covenant in Exodus 25:10.

15

Figure 4

When the *Ark of the Covenant* is pictured (figure 3), it means old Testament worship or the presence of God. When *Noah's Ark* is used (figure 4), it stands for salvation or more particularly the salvation which the Church affords. Thus it is often used as a symbol of the Church.

As these symbols are now used, they should be included in group II.

DOVE—Peace
Genesis 8:11

Figure 5

A *dove* with an *olive branch* in its beak is the symbol of peace. This symbol comes from the account of the cessation of the flood recorded in Genesis 8:11. Noah sent out the dove to see whether the flood was receding. When the dove returned with "a freshly plucked olive leaf" in her beak, Noah knew that the waters were receding.

RAINBOW
God's Covenant With Man
Genesis 9:13

Figure 6

Figure 7

According to the author of Genesis 9:13, God chose this symbol himself. Anyone who believes that symbols should not be used in a Christian context should read the ninth chapter of Genesis. There we find God telling Noah that the *rainbow* shall be a sign of the *covenant* which he is making with mankind (figure 6). God specifically states that the *rainbow shall be a sign* of his promise that "the waters shall never again become a flood to destroy all flesh." This may be the interpretation of the author, but he, at least, thought this symbol important enough to put these words into the speech of God himself. The rainbow, then, should remind us that God does care.

When the *rainbow* is shown with *Noah's Ark* (Figure 7), it is a symbol of the Deluge and God's promise. The rainbow in either of its uses falls in group I.

ALTAR OF BURNT OFFERING

Old Testament Sacrifice

Exodus 40:10

Figure 8

Although the altar is of primary importance, in this particular study it is not within our stated limits to discuss its use except where it appears as a depicted symbol. Such use customarily falls into one of two groups. The *Altar of Burnt Offering* is symbolic of Old Testament sacrifice and is often pictured with smoke ascending as if from the burning offering. The altar with the cross and two or more candles is usually a symbol of the Sacrament of Holy Communion. (*See* chapter VII, pages 65, 66.)

There are over four hundred and fifty references to the altar in the Bible, and most of these have reference to the Altar of Burnt Offering. However, in all of these the emphasis is upon the altar as an entity, not as a symbol. It is the passage of time only that has caused us to symbolize the act of Old Testament sacrifice by picturing an altar. This growth and slow change put the altar in group III or with those symbols that express ideas that are biblical but are not used in that sense in the scriptures.

17

BABEL, TOWER OF
Sinful Presumption
Genesis 11:4-9

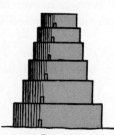

Figure 9

The story of the building of the *Tower of Babel* and the resulting confusion of tongues is a familiar one. This event, which is described in Genesis 11:4-9, is a fitting symbol for man's sinful presumption. This symbol belongs either to group I or II, or to both.

CENSER—Worship
Leviticus 16:12

Figure 10

The censer with its sweet-smelling savor was used in worship services from the earliest times. Thus a burning *censer* has come naturally to signify worhip, adoration, prayer. Bible references may be found in Leviticus 16:12 and Revelation 8:3. This symbol is naturally in group II.

CHERUBIM—Angelic Host
Exodus 25:18-20

Figure 11

It may seem to be a bit indefinite to define *cherubim* as being symbolic of angels. Yet we are driven to indefiniteness by the very nature of angels. Angels, cherubim, and various other beings that can be seen with only the mind's eye appear throughout the Bible. However, there is no scriptural proof that angels are adults and cherubim are children. In fact, early Christian art pictured cherubim with great dignity. Showing them as chubby infants is a later development. These figures are usually shown in connection with a particular event, but whatever the rendition, they are man's

18

feeble attempt to bridge the gap between heaven and earth.

Cherubim as symbols should be in group I because in Exodus 25:18-20 and other places, God commands them to be constructed for the Tabernacle. Their presence there was also symbolic. Cherub is the singular of Cherubim.

HARP—Praise
Psalm 33:2

A representation of the *harp* or lyre is a symbol of praise or worship. This symbol is particularly appropriate on exposed organ pipes or on the choir-bench ends.

The command in Psalm 33:2 to "Praise the Lord with the lyre, make melody to him with the harp of ten strings!" puts this symbol either in group I or II, or in both.

Figure 12

BALANCES—Justice
Daniel 5:27

A set of *balances* is usually the symbol of justice or judgment. Such a symbol reminds us of the story of the Feast of Belshazzar and the interpretation Daniel gives of the handwriting on the wall. "You have been weighed in the balances and found wanting. . . ." Since this particular incident has perhaps resulted in the use of this symbol, it should be included in group II.

Figure 13

BANNER—Victory
Psalm 60:4

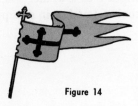

In general a *banner* or as we call it, a "pennant flag," symbolizes victory, triumph, and rejoicing. Since the Resurrection is one of the greatest causes for rejoicing, a banner is often

Figure 14

19

used to remind us of this great truth. The "banner of victory" which we find mentioned in Psalm 60:4 is used in connection with the Lamb to signify the Risen Lord. (*See* Lamb.)

The banner is in group II because it is mentioned in scripture in the same context and with the apparent meaning of victory.

LAMP—Christian Knowledge or Learning
Psalm 119:105

Figure 15

Psalm 119:105 says, "Thy word is a lamp to my feet and a light to my path." What, then, could be more symbolic of Christian knowledge than a *lamp?* The usage illustrated in this verse in Psalms puts this symbol in group I. (*See* also Candle.)

FISH—Jonah
Jonah 1:17

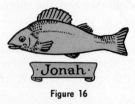

Figure 16

One of the most popular Bible scenes of the catacombs is that which pictures the story of Jonah. Thus, sometimes when a *fish* is used as a symbol, it is to remind us of the story of Jonah. For fish used as an acrostic to symbolize Jesus, *see* Fish in Chapter IV. The fish that swallowed Jonah is not described in the scripture as a whale. The word used means "great fish." This symbol of Jonah is in group II. (*See,* also, Apostles, Andrew.)

CHAPTER III

SYMBOLS OF GOD THE FATHER

In the Beginning God

JESUS was not the first to call God *Father*, but he was the first really to live with God as his father. Yet Jesus came from a group of people who believed that the name of God, *Yahweh*—or as we incorrectly render it, *Jehovah*—was too sacred to utter. In fact, strict Orthodox Jews refrain from speaking this most holy name of God even today. The realization of the fatherliness of the Creator was then and is today of great importance. Perhaps we as sinful humans do need the fear of God to spur us on. Jonathan Edwards at least thought so. He preached his famous sermon, "Sinners in the Hands of an Angry God," many times. But what could be more awful than being a sinner in the hands of a *loving* God, a God whose grief at our punishment is even greater than our own! Jesus revealed God to us as such a Being.

How completely we have failed to grasp Jesus' concept of God the Father may be seen by the fact that in the symbols under this heading only one suggests the fatherly love which God has for us. The Hebrew word which is translated "Almighty" reminds us of God's might. *Yahweh* and *The Lord* are two other names whose exact meanings have been lost in antiquity. The "All-seeing Eye" reminds us of God's continual watchfulness, and the "Hand of God" shows his activities in creating and sustaining the universe. However, the "Hand of God in Blessing" shows that God not only creates but that he also loves and blesses. The two forms, the Latin and the Greek, are of much more recent origin than the other symbols; but they express one of God's most wonderful attributes. It is no accident that the name of Christ is closely connected with both.

In the beginning God was the Father, also.

EL SHADDAI
Genesis 17:1

Figure 17

The Hebrew words *El Shaddai* are translated now to mean "The Almighty." In Genesis 17:1, God speaks to Abraham saying, "I am God Almighty. . . ." Abraham dared to believe, without any human precedent for it, that his God was *All*-mighty and not just a local deity as so many primitives believed. This symbol reminds us, then, that God is all-powerful.

YAHWEH
Exodus 3:15

Figure 18

Other words from the Hebrew used in a similar manner as symbols for God are "Yahweh" and "The Lord." The Jews considered the name *Yahweh*, or Jehovah as we incorrectly render it, too sacred to be even pronounced inside the Temple (figure 18). When they came to the written word *Yahweh*, they did not say it. Instead, they used the words *Adonai* or *El Shaddai*. *Adonai* means "The Lord" (figure 19).

Figure 19

The rays of light surrounding the names when they are used as symbols indicate divinity.

If we agree that names are themselves symbols of the person named, then symbols seventeen, eighteen, and nineteen are included in group I because all of them are scriptural.

EYE, THE ALL-SEEING
Psalm 33:18

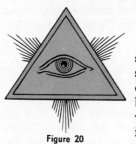

Figure 20

The *All-Seeing Eye* is a very stern symbol that reminds us of the constant scrutiny of God. Being reminded of this aspect of God's personality may be disconcerting to some people, but we should remember that he watches in love and not in condemnation. If we fear for God to know our every action, which of course he does, perhaps our actions are not Christian. This symbol is in group I because it is used many times in the Bible as a reminder of God and his omniscience.

HAND OF GOD
Joshua 4:24

Figure 21

Figure 22

There are more than one hundred references to the *hand of God* in the Bible. Almost every book in the Bible mentions it at least once. Several of them refer to it a great number of times. Is it any wonder, then, that this is one of the oldest and the main symbol of God the Father? Some of these references, chosen at random, are: Exodus 15:6, Numbers 11:23, Deuteronomy 2:15, Joshua 4:24, Ezra 8:18, Nehemiah 2:8, Job 12:9, Ecclesiastes 2:24, Isaiah 11:11, Jeremiah 1:9, Ruth 1:13, II Samuel 24:14, and I Peter 5:6.

The hand is almost always shown surrounded by the *cruciform nimbus*. This shows that the symbol pictured is that of one of the members of the Trinity. Often this symbol is called *Dextra Domini*, meaning the right hand of God. This symbol is also re-

23

Figure 23

ferred to by the Latin words, *Manus Dei,* which mean "The Hand of God" (figure 21).

Very often the hand is shown extended in blessing. There are two main forms of this. The *Latin form* shows the thumb and the first two fingers open and the last two fingers closed. The thumb and the first two fingers stand for the threefold nature of the blessing: "The blessing of God Almighty, the Father, the Son, and the Holy Spirit" (figure 22.)

The second one, the *Greek* type, used especially by the Eastern Church, shows the first finger straight, which stands for *I,* the Greek capital letter for *Iota;* the second finger is curved to form the Greek capital letter *C,* which is the old form of the capital letter for *Sigma* (equal to our letter *S*); the third finger is crossed by the thumb to make the letter *X,* which is the Greek letter *Chi* (equivalent to our *ch*); and the fourth finger is curved like the second to make another *C.* The *IC XC* thus formed is an abbreviation of the name Ἰησοῦς Χριστός, which are the Greek words for Jesus Christ. Thus God blesses the people by the life of Christ (figure 23).

It is not uncommon to see pictures of various Bible characters as well as more recent persons with their hands held in one of these two ways. The Hand of God is in group I. When shown in one of its specialized gestures, it would be either in group I or II, or in both.

24

CHAPTER IV

SYMBOLS OF GOD THE SON

That They May Have Life

THIS is by far the largest chapter of this book. Size does not always signify value, but in this instance it illustrates the fact that Jesus has caused more Christian symbols to arise than any other person. His life and teachings have through the ages inspired men to form symbols in order that they might tell of the Christ. Why? Is he really that important? An examination of these symbols will give at least an inkling of an answer. As mentioned in the previous chapter, Christ's great contribution was that he showed us what God is like. Many of the pictures the Old Testament gives us of God represent him as not being so good as man. But surely man cannot be expected to be better than God. Christ, then, brought our eyes into focus concerning God.

Another thing Jesus did that helps us is this: he proved that it is possible to forget self and yet to win. One cannot seriously consider Jesus' life, death, and resurrection without being moved to do great and noble things for Christ and others. Our emphasis needs to be, as his was, on others. As we come to know Christ better, he helps us to think more of others. With this in mind, examine carefully and prayerfully these symbols, remembering that he said, "I came that they may have life, and have it abundantly."

STAR

Matthew 2:1, 2

There are two main stars used in Christian symbolism, and each has its own special meaning. First, there is the *Creator's Star*. This star has six points and is made by placing one equilateral triangle point downward over another of the same size whose apex is up. The triangles are symbolic of the Trinity.

Figure 24

Such usage reminds us that all three Persons of the Trinity were present and active in creation. This is stated concerning Christ in John 1:1-18. The origin of this star is unknown, but it is very old. It is known to Jewish people as the Star of David or the Shield of David. The six points are said to refer to the attributes of God: power, wisdom, majesty, love, mercy, and justice (figure 24).

Figure 25

The second of these better-known stars is five-pointed and is called variously: the *Star of Epiphany,* the Star of Jacob, the Star of Jesse, or the Star of Bethlehem. See Numbers 24:17; Isaiah 60:3; Matthew 2:1, 2; II Peter 1:19; and Revelation 22:16.

Its most common use is as the *Star of Epiphany.* Epiphany is the time that the Christ Child was shown to the wise men, who represent the Gentiles. According to tradition this occurred twelve days after his birth. Therefore, it is incorrect to use this star as a Christmas symbol. Likewise, the common practice of showing the shepherds and the wise men paying tribute to Jesus at the same time is wrong. A close reading of the stories in Matthew and Luke makes this apparent. For example, Matthew 2:11 says concerning the wise men, "and going into the *house,*" while Luke says concerning Jesus' birth, ". . . and laid him in a manger, because there was no place for them in the inn."

This same star is also used as a symbol of Mary. Such is appropriate because the Hebrew form of the name *Mary* is "Miriam" which means "star."

The Creator's Star is in group III and the Star of Epiphany in group II. When a star is used to symbolize Mary, this symbol falls either in group II or III, or in both.

SCALLOP SHELL—Jesus' Baptism
Mark 1:9-11

Figure 26

Matthew 3:13-17, Luke 3:21, 22, and Mark 1:9-11 describe the baptism of Jesus by John. One of the earliest symbols of this event is a scallop shell with drops of water falling from it. Very old paintings show John pouring water on the head of Jesus from a shell of this type. This symbol is in group III.

Figure 27

DESCENDING DOVE, CHI RHO
Jesus' Baptism
Matthew 3:13-17

Another common symbol of the baptism of Jesus is formed by combining the symbols for the Holy Spirit, for Christ, and for water. Matthew, Mark, and Luke refer to the Holy Spirit descending "as" or "like a dove" on Jesus at his baptism. Therefore the *descending dove,* the *Chi Rho* (*See* pages 36, 37.), and *wavy lines* are used to symbolize this event in Jesus' life. This symbol is in group III.

Figure 28

CHI RHO ON MOUNTAIN
Sermon on the Mount
Matthew 5:1, 2

The gospel of Matthew records Jesus' teachings which we call the Sermon on the Mount as having been given on top of a mountain. Luke 6:17 reports it as having been given on a level place. Following Matthew's account, a *Chi Rho* (*XP*) *on top of a mountain* is used to symbolize these teachings found in Matthew 5:1 through 7:29. These verses include Jesus' most im-

27

portant teachings, including the Beatitudes, the Lord's Prayer, and the Golden Rule. This symbol is in group II or III.

Figure 29

WHEAT AND TARES
Parable of the Weeds
Matthew 13:24-30

Read Matthew 13:24-30 for the facts in Jesus' Parable of the Weeds or Tares. As weeds cannot be gathered up without rooting up also the wheat, so Jesus teaches in this parable that in the Church it is wisest to let the hypocrites grow among the Christians. God will make, in time, the needed separation. Since this symbol of the *wheat and tares* is used metaphorically in the scriptures, it is included in group I.

Figure 30

IHC, TABLETS OF STONE, WHEEL
Transfiguration of Jesus
Luke 9:28

Matthew 17:1-8, Mark 9:2-8, and Luke 9:28-36 all describe the Transfiguration of Jesus. Each seems to be at a loss for words, but they all agree that an intense brightness or whiteness surrounded Jesus. Luke says also that Moses and Elijah "appeared in glory." One of the best symbols for this marvelous meeting is the *glory* which is depicted in figure 129. Another is that which is shown here. It is made of two *tablets of stone* for Moses, a flaming *chariot wheel* for Elijah, and the *IHC* monogram for Jesus (*See* pages 37, 38). This symbol for the Transfiguration is in group II.

Figure 31

PALM BRANCHES
Triumphal Entry and Victory
John 12:13

The figurative language of Revelation 7:9 describes a great multitude of people standing before the throne of the Lamb, clad in white robes and carrying palm branches in their hands. Long before the book of Revelation was written, however, the palm tree or its branches were being used as religious symbols. Victor Schultze says, "Roses, branches of bloom, flowering meadows, and trees, especially the palm, represent paradise, the entrance being indicated by two pillars, or, later, by two great candlesticks." II Chronicles 3:5 and I Kings 7:36 say that the walls and doors of the Temple were decorated with a palm tree motif. These uses are thought to be symbolic of paradise.

Another place that palm branches are prominently used in scripture is in the account of Jesus' Triumphal Entry into Jerusalem described in John 12:13. Because of this account, this day has come to be known as Palm Sunday, and *palm branches* have come to stand for victory.

In the decoration of the Temple and in the Triumphal Entry the palm branches were used symbolically. This makes the palm branch symbol eligible for group I.

Figure 32

BRONZE SERPENT
Type of Crucifixion
John 3:14, 15

The bronze serpent is described in Numbers 21:9, "So Moses made a bronze serpent, and set it on a pole; and if a serpent bit any man, he would look at the bronze serpent and live." It is used by Jesus in John 3:14, 15 to illustrate the way he must be lifted

29

up. He says, "And as Moses lifted up the serpent in the wilderness, so must the Son of man be lifted up, that whoever believes in him may have eternal life." Because of this use, the *bronze serpent* is known symbolically as a type of Jesus' crucifixion. When used in a Christian context, it illustrates his crucifixion. Since Jesus used it metaphorically, it is to be put in group I. (*See* also Snake, Apple, and Apostles, John.)

Figure 33

Figure 34

Figure 35

CHALICE—Holy Communion
Matthew 26:27

Just as the unselfish manner in which Jesus died transformed the cross from a symbol of shame into a supreme symbol of God's love, the special use to which he put the common drinking cup has made of the chalice one of the finest of Christian symbols. When shown alone, the *chalice* stands for faith or worship (figure 33). When used with a communion wafer, it symbolizes Holy Communion (figure 34).

The chalice is also used with the *Crux Acuta,* meaning the Cross of Agony, to symbolize the agony of Christ in Gethsemane (figure 35). (*See* this chapter, Passion Cross.)

The various uses of the chalice may be better understood by referring to Matthew 20:22, 26:27, 26:39; Mark 14:23; and Luke 22:17.

The chalice in its various combinations falls more completely in group II than in any other group. (*See* also Apostles, John.)

CROSS—Passion Cross
Mark 15:20-34

Figure 36

The Gospels of Matthew, Mark, and Luke all record the scene in the Garden of Gethsemane where Jesus is sorely troubled. He was apparently trying to decide whether he could do God's will most completely by going to the cross or by fleeing in order that he might continue teaching. Luke 22:44 says, "And being in an agony he prayed more earnestly; and his sweat became like great drops of blood falling down upon the ground." One can feel the sharp reality of the cross in this scene. Thus a *cross* with its ends cut to points reminds us of this scene in Gethsemane and of Christ's sufferings during the crucifixion. When used with a *chalice,* it even more poignantly reminds us of his suffering in the Garden of Gethsemane. (*See* Chalice.) When portrayed as shown here, it includes all the suffering and shame connected with the crucifixion. It is then rightly called the Passion Cross or Cross of Suffering.

It is shown here instead of in the larger section on crosses because of its particular connection with a special event in the life and death of Jesus. As a symbol it falls into group II.

BAG OF MONEY—Christ's Betrayal
Matthew 26:14-16

Figure 37

A *bag of money* alone or with *30 coins* is the symbol of the betrayal of Jesus by Judas Iscariot. Matthew 26:14-16 records the number of the coins, while Mark 14:10, 11 and Luke 22:3-6 merely say that they promised to give him money. (*See* also Apostles, Judas Iscariot.)

If three bags are pictured, this usually stands for the Apostle Matthew since he was a tax collector. (*See* Apostles, Matthew.)

The symbol of betrayal listed above belongs in group II.

31

LANTERN—Christ's Betrayal
John 18:3

Figure 38

When the Roman soldiers, according to John, went into the Garden of Gethsemane to capture Jesus, they carried lanterns to light their way. For that reason, a *lantern,* usually of octagonal shape, has come to be the symbol of Christ's betrayal and capture. This is the only place in the Bible that the word *lanterns* is used. This symbol belongs in group II.

SCOURGE—Christ's Suffering
Mark 15:15

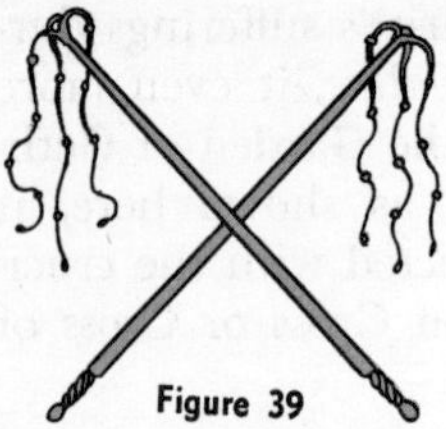

Figure 39

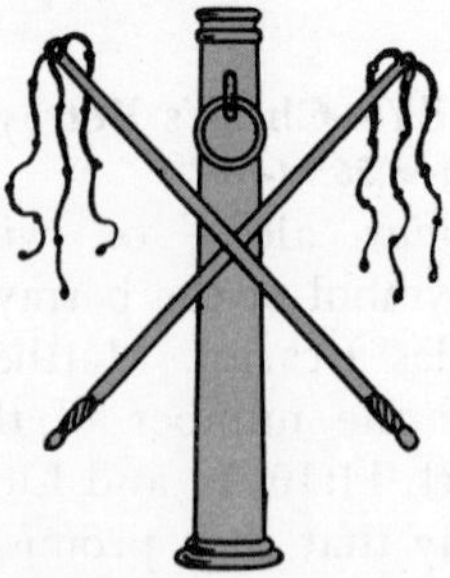

Figure 40

Scourging was the ancient counterpart of our modern practice of giving a prisoner the "third degree." Of course all scourging was not to gain information. Some was merely for punishment; but for whatever reason it was inflicted, it could be a very painful ordeal. The whips or scourges were somewhat similar to our present "cat-o'-nine-tails." The cords attached to the handle were usually knotted and had bits of bone or lead tied at the ends. These would cause cuts in addition to the ridges raised by the ordinary whipcord.

Since scourging was very painful, the prisoner was often tied to a post to keep him from falling or running away. Matthew 27:26 and Mark 15:15 tell of Jesus being scourged. The scourge or whip has for that reason come to be a symbol of Christ's suffering just prior to the crucifixion. Often *two scourges* are shown arranged in the shape of an X.

Figure 41

A *column* or whipping post is also commonly combined with the *scourges*. Sometimes the column only is shown with a *ring* to which the prisoner's hands were tied. These symbols reveal the failure of brutal force to solve man's problems. Either arrangement is symbolic of Christ's suffering and puts this symbol in group II.

CROWN OF THORNS
Christ's Suffering
Matthew 27:29

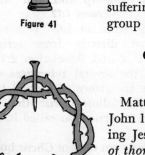

Figure 42

Matthew 27:29, Mark 15:17, and John 19:2 all tell of the soldiers mocking Jesus by placing a plaited *crown of thorns* on his head. This symbol is often combined with the three or four nails supposedly used to nail Jesus to the cross (figure 42). Either or both symbolize the torture and crucifixion of our Lord. Sometimes the initials *I. N. R. I.* are placed inside the circle formed by the thorns (figure 43). These are also used alone and are an abbreviation of the inscription which was placed on the cross over the head of Jesus. The inscription, which is mentioned in Matthew 27:37 and Luke 23:38, is complete only in John

Figure 43

19:19. The Roman letters, *I. N. R. I.,* are the abbreviation for the Latin words, *Iesus Nazarenus Rex Iudaeorum.* Translated into English, they mean "Jesus of Nazareth, the King of the Jews."

33

The crown of thorns was placed on Jesus' head as a mockery of his supposed kingship. Since history has proved his right to the office, this symbol proves the point that sometimes fools are better prophets than the wise. This cruel crown should be in group I because it was used symbolically in scripture. The same is true of *I. N. R. I.*

CROWN
Christ's Kingship and Our Reward
James 1:12

Figure 44

"The crown of life" is a symbol borrowed directly from scripture. James 1:12 and Revelation 2:10 are two of the several references which promise the crown of eternal life to those who follow Christ, the "King of kings." Christ is so called in Revelation 17:14 and 19:16.

The *crown,* therefore, reminds us not only of Christ but also of the kingly office which all Christians must fill. Since the phrase "crown of life" is used symbolically or metaphorically in scripture, this symbol belongs in group I.

CANDLE—Christ
John 8:12

Figure 45

Candles are a relatively recent invention. They were not used in Palestine prior to A.D. 100. The words that are translated *candle* and *candlestick* in the King James Version are more correctly translated *lamp* and *lampstand* in the Revised Standard Version. So the symbol which the candle replaces is a lamp. Low bowls holding oil and a wick were used for light during biblical times. Thus, by a process of substitution, the candle has come into common use as a symbol of Jesus Christ, "the light of the world." Therefore, we use candles on our altar or communion table to remind us of the words found in John 8:12 and 9:5: "I am the light of the world."

The practice of using two candles, and thus two candlesticks, probably arose from the necessity of balancing one with the other, since the cross should have the central place. However, the two are exceedingly expressive of the twofold nature of our Lord, his human nature and his divine nature. Scriptural justification for the use of this particular method to express this great truth cannot be found since candles were not used in Palestine prior to A.D. 100. This symbol is in group III.

Figure 46

Figure 47

Figure 48

ALPHA AND OMEGA

Eternalness of Christ

Revelation 22:13

Alpha (A) and *Omega* (Ω is the capital letter and ω the small) are the first and last letters in the Greek alphabet. When they are used together, they have a similar meaning to our expression, "from A to Z." They stand for the beginning and the end, the first and the last.

The best illustration of the scriptural use of these symbols is Revelation 22:13. They are also used in the same sense in Revelation 1:8 and 21:6. Since these are designed to show the eternalness of Christ, they should always be used in connection with a monogram or some other symbol that signifies Christ; otherwise, their meaning would be simply two letters of the Greek alphabet.

35

Some of the symbols or monograms used with these are: Alpha and the Budded Cross (figure 46); Alpha, Omega, and Crown (figure 47); Alpha, Omega, and Chi Rho (figure 48); Alpha, Omega, and Cross of Suffering (figure 49); and Omega and the Latin Cross (figure 50).

This symbol falls into group I, that is, with those which are specifically used in the Bible.

Figure 49

Figure 50

Figure 51

CHI RHO (XP)—Christ

The *XP* symbol is one of the most ancient of all the monograms used to remind us of Christ. This, as well as several others, is actually an abbreviation or a contraction but for the sake of convenience may be included in the group called monograms.

Many of the early Christian manuscripts were written in Greek capital letters or uncials, as they are called technically. Thus, when the name Christ was written in Greek uncials, it appeared as *XPICTOC*. The *C* is the old method of writing the Greek capital letter *Sigma*. By taking the first two letters of this word

36

Figure 52

Figure 53

Figure 54

XPICTOC, we get the symbol which is called the *Chi Rho.* A horizontal line or *vinculum* should always be placed over this and any other monogram that is a contraction to show that it is an abbreviation or contraction. *See* figures 51 and 52 for two different forms of the Chi Rho. Figure 53 is the Chi Rho Sigma.

Like most of the monograms, this symbol is not specified by the scriptures, but rather arose from a study of them in the original tongue. It is, therefore, in group III.

IHC or IHS—Jesus
Acts 4:12

In our Protestant churches this symbol is probably seen more often than any other except the cross. The *IHC* form is older and more authentic than the *IHS.* There is widespread ignorance regarding its correct meaning. Two common interpretations that are definitely wrong are that the symbol stands for "in His Service"; and *Jesus Hominum Salvator,* Latin for "Jesus, Savior of Mankind." It is believed that a Franciscan monk, Saint Bernadine of Siena (A.D. 1380-1444), was responsible for the latter unauthentic interpretation.

37

Figure 55

Figure 56

Actually, these three letters are an abbreviation for the name *Jesus* in Greek. Since this is an abbreviation, it should be shown with a horizontal line, *vinculum,* over it. This signifies that it is an abbreviation or contraction. It is incorrect to use periods after each letter, as these are not initials but are the first three letters of the Greek word in capitals for Jesus, *IHCOYC.* (For a discussion of Greek letters see Fish and Hand.) The symbol is also often written in minuscules or small Greek letters. The *H* in this symbol is the capital letter for *Eta,* which is the Greek letter equivalent to our letter *E.* The *C* is the old form of the Greek capital for *Sigma.*

The Hebrew, Latin, or Greek words, from which our biblical words are derived, are just as scriptural as the words in our English Bible. In fact, they are often more correct than ours since we get many of our words from them. To use such words correctly is evidence of an alert mind. (*See* figure 54 for *IHC;* figures 55, 56 for forms of *IHS.*)

The abbreviation *IHC* reminds us of the name *Jesus* and the life that Jesus lived. This symbol is in group III.

FISH—Jesus

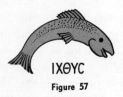

IXΘYC

Figure 57

The scriptural origin of this symbol is somewhat obscure. But it may have arisen from the story in Luke 24:42 about Jesus eating a piece of fish after the resurrection. The *fish* was used by the persecuted Christians as a method of conveying a message to other Christians without the message being understood by the Roman police. In *Christian Symbolism in the Evangelical Churches,* Thomas Stafford says of this symbol, "When displayed outside a pagan home, it indicated that a funeral banquet was being held for the dead, but when it appeared outside a Christian home, it was a sign that the Lord's Supper would be celebrated there, at night, in secret."

The Greek word *fish*—IXΘYC in capital letters, ἰχθύς in small Greek letters—can be made into an acrostic by regarding each letter in it as the initial of a word in the sentence, "Jesus Christ, Son of God, Savior." Taking the Greek word for fish, IXΘYC, let the letters represent thus:

I stands for the Greek word for *Jesus,* Ἰησοῦς,

X represents the Greek word for *Christ,* χριστὸς,

Θ represents the Greek word for *of God,* Θηοῦ,

Y stands for the Greek word for *Son,* Υἱὸς,

C or Σ stands for the Greek word for *Savior,* Σωτήρ.

A word of explanation may be necessary for those who do not know Greek. Our *J* is the nearest equivalent for the Greek I. The letter that appears to be an *n* in the Greek is the Greek letter Eta (η) or roughly the equivalent of our letter *e.* The Greek letter *Sigma* is written in three different ways. Besides the three different ways it is written, symbolism continues to use the old form for writing the capital Greek letter for *Sigma,* C. The capital used today for Sigma is Σ. When a Sigma appears inside a word as a minuscule or small letter, it is written σ; but when it appears at the end of a word, it is written ς. This acrostic use of the fish falls into group III.

Figure 58

EASTER LILY—Resurrection

There is no specific scriptural justification for using the *Easter lily* as a symbol, but it does aptly describe our hope in the resurrection. When the bulb is buried in the earth, out of it grows foliage and a new bulb. This symbolizes the gaining of immortal life by the death of the body. The *Madonna lily,* which is the

39

same as that described above, is also the symbol of Mary the mother of Jesus. It typifies purity and innocence. In this connection it is also used to symbolize the Annunciation, the announcement to the virgin Mary, as recorded in Luke 1:31, that she is to bear a child. These symbols are in group III.

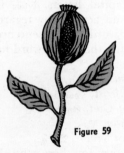

Figure 59

POMEGRANATE—Resurrection
II Chronicles 3:16

The pomegranate is mentioned in Exodus 28:34, Numbers 13:23, Deuteronomy 8:8, I Samuel 14:2, I Kings 7:42, II Kings 25:17, II Chronicles 3:16, Song of Solomon 4:3, Jeremiah 52:23, Joel 1:12, and Haggai 2:19. In fact, many of these references describe some piece of wearing apparel of the priest or a furnishing of the Tabernacle and tell how pomegranates should be embroidered on them. I Kings 7:42, for example, tells how there were four hundred pomegranates on the network that was used to cover the bowls which sat on top of the two pillars outside the Temple. To the early Hebrews the pomegranate probably stood for fecundity or reproductive power. To the present-day Christian it stands for the resurrection of Christ and also for the resurrection of his followers. When the pomegranate ripens, the seeds burst out. Just as the jacket is not able to hold the seed, neither was the grave able to hold Jesus. The application of the resurrection idea to the Old Testament symbol puts the pomegranate either in group I or II, or in both.

Figure 60

BUTTERFLY—Resurrection

This symbol is not scriptural, but is beautifully expressive of the Christian's belief in the resurrection because of the fact that the butterfly ceases to be a worm before it becomes a lovely butterfly.

The stages of development in the

life of a *butterfly* suggest an amazing parallel to the various stages in the life of a Christian. The butterfly goes from the crawling larva stage to the pupa or chrysalis stage, in which it is so dormant that it appears lifeless. Then it comes forth the beautiful soaring butterfly. The Christian first as a mortal man lives a lowly life; then he enters death, that which appears the end; but he is raised into the greatest gift God has to impart, eternal life through faith in Jesus Christ. This symbol falls, of course, in group III.

PEACOCK
Immortality and Resurrection

Figure 61

There is a very old pre-Christian legend that says that the flesh of the peacock never decays but always remains sweet and fresh. For that reason it has been adopted by Christians as a symbol of immortality or resurrection. This early belief must have been widespread, for John P. Lundy quotes Augustine's comment upon this belief in the never-decaying nature of peacock flesh.

Another reason, and the main one, the peacock symbol fits this idea so well is that when he molts he grows new feathers more brilliant than those which he lost. This reminds us that new life gained by death is better even than the old life.

There is no specific scriptural justification for the use of the peacock as a symbol; therefore it falls in group III.

PHOENIX—Resurrection

Figure 62

One of the first accounts of this legendary bird, the *phoenix*, is that written by Herodotus about the fifth century B.C. Many authors have written about the phoenix since that time, and all of the accounts do not agree. But, in general, they do agree that the phoenix was a large bird with gorgeous plumage and was the only one of its

41

kind. It was always male and lived to be about 500 years old. At the end of this time, it always built a nest of spice twigs and burned itself alive by setting the nest on fire. Then it would rise again with renewed youth from its own ashes.

Today the legend is, of course, not considered true. But it does remind us of the true story of the resurrection. It serves as a symbol of this and should be put in group III.

Figure 63

THE GOOD SHEPHERD—Christ
John 10:11

In John 10:11 Jesus says, "I am the good shepherd. The good shepherd lays down his life for the sheep." Again in John 10:14, 15 he says, "I am the good shepherd; I know my own and my own know me, as the Father knows me and I know the Father; and I lay down my life for the sheep." These verses and the life of service that Jesus lived and the sacrificial death that he died have inspired the figure of a stalwart young man carrying a lamb on his shoulders to become a symbol of Christ. This symbol is in group I.

Figure 64

LAMB—Christ
John 1:29

According to John 1:29, when John the Baptist saw Jesus, he said, "Behold, the Lamb of God." This and a similar statement in John 1:36 have brought into being two of our most meaningful symbols of Jesus Christ. One form of this symbol shows a lamb reclining on the Book of the Seven Seals mentioned in Revelation 5:1 (figure 64). Another form, known as the *Triumphant Lamb*, shows a lamb

Figure 65

standing with an unfurled banner waving over it (figure 65.) . Both of these symbols are called *Agnus Dei,* which is Latin for "Lamb of God." The banner that the standing Lamb holds symbolizes Christ's victory over death. (*See* Banner.)

Since John the Baptist was the forerunner of Christ and was the first to use this terminology to speak of Christ, a form of this symbol with the lamb standing on the book is sometimes used as the symbol of this "Wilderness Prophet." Another symbol also used to remind us of John the Baptist is a camel's-hair coat.

The lamb as a symbol of Christ belongs in group II, and as a symbol of John it belongs in group III.

GRIFFIN—Two Natures of Christ

Figure 66

The *griffin* is an imaginary creature that has the wings and beak of an eagle and the body of a lion. This combination signifies to Christians the twofold nature of Christ. The eagle-like portion speaks of his divinity, and the lion-like part reminds us of his humanity.

Since the griffin is not a biblical creature, this symbol belongs in group III.

CHAPTER V

SYMBOLS OF GOD THE HOLY SPIRIT, AND OF THE TRINITY

A Man's Reach Should Exceed His Grasp

THE Holy Spirit is the Comforter and Counselor. He will guide, aid, bless, and keep us if we will only invite him into our hearts and seek his guidance. Where a real Christian is, there the Holy Spirit is also. Those persons who have surrendered themselves to God in an unusual degree show the most evidence of being possessed by the Holy Spirit. His office is that of helping us to know the will of the Father and of the Son. The Holy Spirit also strengthens us for the doing of that will.

The Trinity is: God the Father, God the Son, and God the Holy Spirit. These three Persons of one nature are commonly referred to as Father, Son, and Holy Spirit. When all three are combined, they form the Godhead or Trinity. Trinity literally means "three in one."

With our present knowledge it is not possible for us to understand how the Godhead can be one yet three at the same time. We are limited by time and space. God is not so limited. He is able to know the future; our knowledge is mainly limited to the past. We see in a mirror dimly and reason from our limited view. It is an intimation of man's immortality that he can come to a conclusion which transcends his logic:

> "Ah, but a man's reach should exceed his grasp,
> Or what's a heaven for?"

THE HOLY SPIRIT

DOVE

Matthew 3:16

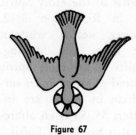

Figure 67

It is a rare thing when all four of the Gospels describe the same event. It is even rarer when they describe the same event in similar words. However, in reporting the Holy Spirit's descent upon Jesus, all four say that it came *as* or *like* a dove from heaven. See Matthew 3:16, Mark 1:10, Luke 3:22, and John 1:32. Thus the *dove* has come to be the most widely recognized symbol of the Holy Spirit.

SEVEN-TONGUED FLAME

Acts 2:1-4

Figure 68

Another symbol that is also used to depict the Holy Spirit is a *seven-tongued flame*. This is based on the story of Pentecost as it is recorded in the second chapter of Acts.

Figure 69

SEVEN LAMPS

Revelation 4:5

Seven lamps are also used to remind us of the Holy Spirit. They are referred to in Revelation 4:5 as seven torches of fire, which are the seven spirits of God.

45

SEVEN DOVES
Revelation 5:12

The seven gifts of the Holy Spirit are discussed in Revelation 5:12. They are: power, wealth, wisdom, might, honor, glory, and blessing. These seven gifts of the Holy Spirit are often pictured as *seven doves* surrounding a circle in which are inscribed the letters *SS. SS* is an abbreviation of *Sanctus Spiritus,* which is Latin for "Holy Spirit."

Figure 70

The dove, the seven-tongued flame, and the seven doves are all in group I because they appear in the Bible as symbols of the ideas that lie behind them. The symbol *SS* is difficult to group because it is an abbreviation of the Latin words for "Holy Spirit." These are, of course, scriptural, but the abbreviation itself is not used in the scriptures. It would, therefore, be in group II or III.

THE TRINITY

TRIANGLE

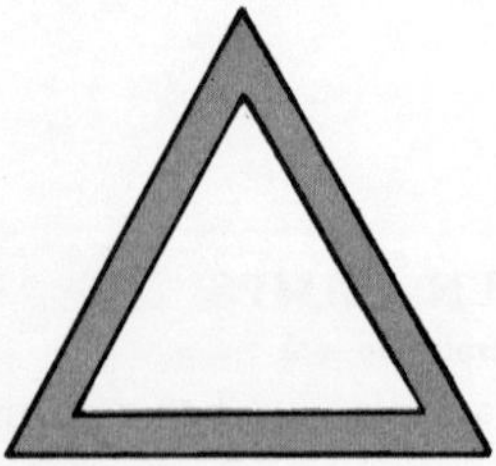

Perhaps the most commonly used symbol of the Trinity is an *equilateral triangle*. This reminds us that all three Persons of the Trinity are distinct, as are the sides of the triangle. Yet all are inseparably joined like the triangle. Since all three sides are of equal length, this reminds us of the equality of the three Persons of the Trinity. The union of these three sides results in one figure which suggests the one and inseparable Godhead.

Figure 71

46

Figure 72

TWO TRIANGLES AND CIRCLE

The *triangle* is used in many different ways and with other symbols, such as the *circle,* to further emphasize various attributes of the Trinity.

Figure 73

THREE INTERWOVEN CIRCLES

The three *interwoven circles* of equal size indicate the equality, eternity, and unity of the three Persons in the Trinity.

Figure 74

TREFOIL AND TRIANGLE

The *trefoil* has the same symbolic meaning as the interwoven circles, and is fashioned by removing all the lines that cross inside the circles.

Figure 75

TRIQUETRA

The *triquetra* is formed from the portions of the circles that are removed in forming the trefoil. In other words, a triquetra and a trefoil combined give you the interwoven circles. However, notice that the triquetra usually has the single point turned upward.

47

Figure 76

Figure 77

THREE FISH

Since a fish was an early symbol used to represent Christ, *three fish* arranged in a triangle symbolize the three members of the Trinity.

FLEUR-DE-LIS

Fleur-de-lis is French for "flower of the lily." This is actually a conventionalized form of the flower that Americans call "iris" or "flag." It is emblematic of the Trinity because of its threefold division. The *Fleur-de-lis* is also an emblem of the purity of the virgin Mary. (*See* Easter Lily.)

Although this is a very old emblem, there seems to be no scriptural basis for its use as a symbol. We get an idea of its age in this use as a symbol from the knowledge that since all three Persons of the Godhead are not shown to be equal, it evidently came into use before the doctrine of their equality arose in the third century, A.D. This symbol is in group III.

Figure 78

SHAMROCK

St. Patrick appeared before the pagan King of Ireland, according to legend, to speak to him about the Holy Trinity. The king could not understand how three persons could be in one. St. Patrick plucked a *shamrock* that was growing near. He showed it to the king, asking him if it were one leaf or three. The king was unable to answer the questions asked him about the shamrock. Then St. Patrick assured him that if he could not explain the mystery of the shamrock, that there was no hope of him understanding so deep a mystery as the Holy Trinity. The shamrock is a well-known symbol of the Trinity.

CHAPTER VI

SYMBOLS OF THE BIBLE AND ITS CHARACTERS

The Map and the Map-Makers

THIS entire book deals with the Bible and the symbols it has inspired. But the symbols of the Bible itself and the persons it tells about require a special chapter.

Unfortunately, it has not been possible to include the symbols of all the famous or infamous scriptural characters. Only the best-known ones are discussed. It is hoped they may introduce the reader to the main players and lead to renewed interest in them and those associated with them.

Take John the Baptist. He was born of ordinary parents in an obscure village. He lived a lonely life far from the things that most of us consider important. His food was gathered from the lean of the land, and his coat was the shaggy skin of a camel. Yet, with a few others, he stands against the horizon of time, saying, "Make straight the way of the Lord."

Try to figure out what made these common men become uncommon in their actions. Take Peter, Paul, or Philip, learn all you can about him. Put yourself in his sandals. Walk with him down the hot, dusty road. To do so will inspire one to be a better person.

BOOK—The Holy Bible

Figure 79

Sir Walter Scott on his deathbed asked for "The Book." Someone questioned him as to the book he desired. He replied, "Need you ask? There is but one." A world-wide appreciation of the Bible such as that expressed by Scott makes the outline of a *book* almost automatically rep-

Figure 80

resent the Holy Bible.

This well-known symbol is often used in connection with that of several others to symbolize certain persons that live through its pages. For example, the open Bible and a sword is a common symbol for the Apostle Paul. (*See* Apostles, Paul and Simon Zelotes.)

Since scrolls were used as books before the *page* method we now use, the *scroll* is also used to signify scripture (figure 80). Sometimes two scrolls are used, one representing the Old Testament and the other representing the New Testament. The scroll is in group III because there is no special mention of such an application and use in scripture.

Figure 81

EVANGELISTS—The Four Gospels

The writer of any one of the four Gospels is referred to as an Evangelist. For many years the early Christians did not agree exactly which symbol should stand for which Evangelist. On pages 185-188 in Webber's *Church Symbolism* is a section dealing with the figures used to symbolize the Evangelists.

Figure 82

As far as their modern use is concerned, the symbols and their meanings are as follows: The *Winged Man* (figure 81) is used to symbolize St. Matthew since he traces the human lineage of Jesus. The *Winged Lion* (figure 82) represents St. Mark because of the reference Mark makes to John the Baptist, "The voice of one crying in the wilderness."

Figure 83

The *Winged Ox* (figure 83) represents St. Luke because he points up the atoning sacrifice of Christ. The *Eagle* (figure 84) is used to symbolize St. John because, like the eagle, his Gospel soars to great heights in expressing the heavenly nature of Christ our Saviour.

Figure 84

These are all in group III because they are devices that are suggested by scripture but not specifically used therein in this way. But references to creatures like these may be found in Ezekiel 1:10 and in Revelation 4:6-8.

Figure 85

CAMEL'S-HAIR TUNIC
John the Baptist
Matthew 3:4

Matthew 3:4 and Mark 1:6 both record the fact that John the Baptist dressed in a camel's-hair garment. Thus a rough, woolly, *camel's-hair coat* has come to be the symbol of this wilderness prophet. This symbol is in group II.

APOSTLES

A symbol that represents a historical character is usually placed upon a shield. This helps to make plain the fact that a particular incident in the person's life is being remembered.

51

The Apostles' symbols are, therefore, herein shown mounted on shields. However, since each of the twelve Apostles has several traditional symbols, it is very difficult to limit their symbolic representation to one shield each.* For the sake of completeness, this book will show more than one shield wherever possible. Since there is not general agreement as to the sequence in which the Apostles should be presented, they will, with the exception of Paul, be arranged alphabetically.

Judas Iscariot is often left out of the group and Paul is put in to complete the number. When both are included, the number is thirteen. When Matthias is added there are fourteen. The number is not too important, but it can serve to illustrate the fact not commonly known that there is not complete agreement as to who the twelve Apostles were. The lists which are found in Mark and Luke do not agree. Nathanael and Bartholomew; Levi and Matthew; and Thaddaeus and Judas, son of James, are thought to be respectively the same persons. This is, however, tradition and cannot be substantiated by scripture.

Figure 86

ANDREW
Matthew 4:18

The most common form of Andrew's shield shows a *Cross Saltire* (figure 86), which is an X-shaped cross with its ends reaching the border of the shield. Tradition has it that Andrew was crucified in Greece on a cross of this sort.

---

* The Upper Room Chapel in Nashville, Tennessee, has on its altar rail beautiful wood carvings of the shields of the Apostles. Pictures of these shields are included in chapter VIII of this book.

Figure 87

Another form shows two fish crossed (figure 87). This recalls his original occupation and his call to become a "fisher of men," as recorded in Matthew 4:19 and Mark 1:17. Since nothing is given in scripture concerning the death of Andrew, the first symbol falls in group III, and the second either in group II or III, or in both.

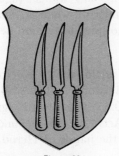

Figure 88

BARTHOLOMEW
John 1:49

This Apostle, thought to be the same as Nathanael, is said to have been flayed alive and then crucified. Thus, *three flaying knives*, knives used for skinning animals, are his most common symbol (figure 88).

Figure 89

An open Bible with a knife is also commonly used. This recalls his faith in God's word, as recorded in John 1:49, as well as the method of his martyrdom. Bartholomew made this confession of faith to Jesus, "Rabbi, you are the Son of God! You are the King of Israel!"

The first symbol of Bartholomew discussed falls in group III, and the second falls in group II.

53

Figure 90

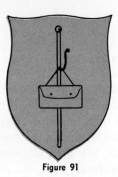

Figure 91

Figure 92

JAMES THE GREATER
Acts 12:2

Because tradition attributes to him wide travels, all of James the Greater's shields are related to pilgrimage and missionary journeys. The more common one shows *three scallop shells* (figure 90). The scallop shell is the symbol of pilgrimage.

Another shield of James the Greater shows a pilgrim's staff upon which is placed a pilgrim's wallet (figure 91). How wonderful when a man's wallet is used to spread the good news of Christ!

The third shield shows a cross-hilted, vertical sword and a scallop shell (figure 92). This sword signifies his death. Acts 12:2 tells of James's martyrdom at the hands of Herod.

The scallop shell is also used as a symbol of baptism. Many early pictures of the baptism of Jesus by John show John pouring water from such a shell on Jesus' head.

Since Acts 12:2 tells of James's martyrdom by Herod and says that he was beheaded, it is reasonable to assume that he was beheaded with a sword. The sword part of his symbol would then fall in group II. However, since the rest of his symbols have arisen from tradition only, they fall in group III.

JAMES THE LESS

Figure 93

This Apostle's most common shield shows a *vertical handsaw* with the handle upward (figure 93). Hegesippus, an early historian, says that at the age of 96 James the Less was taken to the top of the Temple in Jerusalem and pushed off. Although seriously injured, he staggered to his feet, begging God to forgive his enemies. This angered the Jews so that they stoned him and finally killed him with a fuller's bat, a club used to beat clothes in washing. His dead body was then sawed asunder. The fuller's bat is also used as his symbol (figure 94).

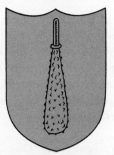

Figure 94

These symbols grew out of tradition and are in group III.

(These symbols have been used for centuries to represent James the son of Alphaeus, one of the twelve apostles. However, research reveals that Hegesippus was writing about "James the brother of the Lord.")

JOHN

Figure 95

John is shown as an apostle and also as one of the Four Evangelists. (For the symbol of John the Evangelist, *see* page 51.) The shield used to represent John has upon it a *chalice* (cup) out of which a *snake* is crawling. Like many other symbols, this arose from tradition. Early writers state that an attempt was made by the priest of Diana to poison John. However, John made the sign of the cross over the chalice and the poison escaped in the form of a serpent. This symbol falls into group III.

Figure 96

JUDAS ISCARIOT
Matthew 26:14, 15

A very common portrayal of Judas is a blank shield of a dirty-yellow color. The tragedy in Judas' life lay in the wrong spirit in his soul that led him to betray the Master. This shield symbolizes the sin-marred life of Judas.

Figure 97

Another shield has *thirty pieces of silver* and a *money bag* (figure 97). Whether or not the money was the deciding influence in the betrayal, the fact is that Judas betrayed Jesus for a very meager price. Money bags and money are often connected with betrayal.

Paradoxically, Jesus, the One betrayed, saves men from falling into the sin of betraying the best.

Figure 98

Another combination of this symbol is thirty pieces of silver and a rope (figure 98). According to Matthew 27:5, Judas hanged himself in remorse over his betrayal of Jesus. This symbol explains the use of the rope on Judas' shield.

These symbols of Judas are included in group II because scripture verses mention the coins and refer to Judas' suicide by hanging.

JUDE

Figure 99

The Apostle Jude, also called Thaddaeus or Lebbaeus, or Judas not Iscariot, is said to have traveled a great deal by ship during his missionary journeys. Thus, a small *ship* at *full sail* is placed on his shield (figure 99).

The ship at full sail is also a symbol of the Church. (*See* Ship.)

Figure 100

A second form of his shield shows a carpenter's square and a boat hook because of his traditional, widespread building activity (figure 100). All of his symbols fall in group III since most of the things we find attributed to Jude come from tradition.

Figure 101

MATTHEW
Matthew 9:9; 10:3

The Gospels of Mark and Luke in recording the call of the tax collector name him Levi. However, the name Levi does not appear in any of the lists of the Apostles that we have in the New Testament. The only tax collector mentioned is Matthew. They

57

Figure 102

are, therefore, thought to be the same person. Thus, the *three money bags* are used to represent Matthew because they depict his previous occupation as told in Matthew 9:9 and 10:3.

A vertical battle-ax is also used to symbolize Matthew (figure 102).

Figure 103

Another shield used to represent Matthew employs a Tau Cross (figure 103). These shields came into use from the tradition that Matthew was crucified in Ethiopia on a Tau Cross and that his head was cut off with a battle-ax. Matthew's first symbol falls in group II and his others in group III.

Figure 104

MATTHIAS

The Apostle Matthias was made one of the twelve Apostles by being chosen to take the place of Judas Iscariot. His most common shield is an *open Bible* and a *double battle-ax* of a primitive type (figure 104).

58

Figure 105

Another shield for Matthias shows a battle-ax and two stones (figure 105). Both of these symbols arose from the tradition that Matthias was stoned and then beheaded for preaching the gospel in Judea. His symbols fall into group III.

PETER
Matthew 16:13-19

Figure 106

Peter's most commonly used shield shows two large *keys saltire,* that is, crossed like the letter X (figure 106). Justification for the use of the keys as a symbol for Peter may be found in Matthew 16:13-19.

Figure 107

Another shield that is commonly used to represent Peter shows an inverted Latin Cross (figure 107). According to tradition, Peter requested that he be crucified head downward because he did not think himself worthy of dying in the same manner as his Lord.

59

Figure 108

These two former figures, the two keys saltire, and the inverted Latin Cross are also often combined to form a shield for Peter. This interesting combination suggests the truth that it is through the cross of Christ that the door into the kingdom of heaven is opened for us.

Figure 109

A fourth shield used to represent Peter reminds us of his denial of his Lord. It pictures the crowing of the cock as told in Matthew 26:75, Mark 14:72, and Luke 22:60 (figure 109).

The first symbol falls either into group I or II, or in both. The second is tradition alone; so it belongs in group III. Since the third is a combination, it falls into both group I and group III. The fourth symbol falls in group I because the crowing of the cock was to symbolize to Peter his failure.

Figure 110

PHILIP
John 6:7

Philip is shown symbolically by a *cross* and *two loaves of bread* (figure 110). John 6:7 identifies the Apostle who talked with Jesus about the feeding of the 5,000 as being Philip.

Figure 111

An interesting variation of the loaves of bread is the substitution of stalks of wheat for the loaves (figure 111). This is done on Philip's shield in The Upper Room Chapel in Nashville, Tennessee.

Figure 112

Other shields used to denote Philip are a basket and a Tau Cross (figure 112), and a vertical spear (figure 113). Supposedly, the latter was the instrument of his martyrdom. The symbol discussed first falls into group II and the others in group III.

Figure 113

The Apostle Philip was of a timid and retiring disposition. He was slow of heart and not too keen in his spiritual grasp. But it seems he had talents of a practical nature. From John 6:5-7 it is suggested that he might have been the one who arranged for the provisions for Jesus and the Twelve. These symbols speak of the useful life Philip lived for Christ.

61

SIMON ZELOTES

Figure 114

The most familiar symbol for Simon Zelotes is a *book* upon which lies a *fish* (figure 114). This symbol is given to him because he was a great fisher of men through the power of the gospel of Jesus Christ.

Figure 115

He is said to have been a companion of Jude on many of his journeys. Thus, he is sometimes symbolized by a fish impaled on a boat hook (figure 115). Simon Zelotes' symbols fall in group III.

Figure 116

THOMAS

Thomas was by nature a man of gloom and doubt. He had great difficulty coming to an inner assurance of faith in Christ. But finally he was able to cry with inner certainty, "My Lord and my God."

The shield of the Apostle Thomas shows a *vertical spear* and a *carpenter's square* (figure 116).

Figure 117

Sometimes the square only is used to symbolize Thomas (figure 117). Tradition says that Thomas went to East India as a missionary, and at Malipur built a church with his own hands. While there, he was shot with arrows and finally killed by a pagan priest's spear.

Figure 118

Another variation of the shield of Thomas is to combine the carpenter's square, spear, and four arrows. This symbol speaks of both Thomas' labors and of his death in the service of Christ.

Since all his symbols are supported by tradition alone, they fall into group III.

Figure 119

PAUL
Ephesians 6:16, 17

The most common symbol used to denote Paul is an *open Bible,* the Word of God, behind which can be seen a vertical, *cross-hilted sword.* Across the front of the Bible are the words *Spiritus Gladius,* which mean the "sword of the spirit" (figure 119). In Ephesians 6:17 Paul speaks of the Word of God as being "the sword of the Spirit."

63

Figure 120

Another common method used to symbolize Paul is a rayed Latin Cross (figure 120). This is sometimes called the shield of faith. In Ephesians 6:16 Paul speaks of "taking the shield of faith, with which you can quench all the flaming darts of the evil one." Paul's symbols given here fall into groups I and II.

CHAPTER VII

SYMBOLS OF DOCTRINES, IDEAS, AND SACRAMENTS

Think About These Things

A BRILLIANT theologian once said, "A dogma is a doctrine which has forgotten that it ever had a history." In over-simplified terms, a *dogma* is a belief about which there can be no question. A *doctrine* is a belief about which there is still some speculation, a matter that can be examined historically. The Protestant Church has no dogmas. At least it does not admit to any. However, we are often dogmatic about our doctrines. Such an attitude is a contradiction of terms, logic, and Christianity. Although we are all illogical beings, we should at least try to be as reasonable as possible. The following doctrines, ideas, and sacraments are presented with the hope that as we learn their symbols we may recognize their devotional value. Since symbols are broader than words, a devotional understanding of them may well bring together Christians who are being kept apart by mere terms.

"Finally, brethren, whatever is true, whatever is honorable, whatever is just, whatever is pure, whatever is lovely, whatever is gracious, if there is any excellence, if there is anything worthy of praise, think about these things."

Figure 121

ALTAR—Holy Communion

The use of an altar in Christian churches began after the Bible was written. Its use seems to be a direct borrowing from the usage described in the Old Testament. There we find it used to hold the burnt offering which, according to the Law, had to be offered to God. Christians adapted this idea of the importance of sac-

65

rifice by placing the symbol of Christ upon the altar. This symbolizes the atonement which Christ's death produced. This symbol, the *altar,* has come to be a symbol of the Holy Communion.

The altar as a symbol falls into group III since it expresses an idea that is biblical but is not itself used in that sense in the scriptures.

Figure 122

Figure 123

GRAPES—Holy Communion
Matthew 26:27-29

The most common meaning of a *cluster of grapes,* particularly when it is combined with *sheaves of wheat,* is that of Holy Communion (figure 122). Matthew 26:29, Mark 14:25, and Luke 22:18 all speak of "the fruit of the vine" in their accounts of the Last Supper. *Wheat* also stands for "the bread of life" or Holy Communion (figure 123).

The cluster of grapes and the stalks of wheat are not used in this connection in the Bible. It is their products that are so used. In keeping with our classification of the various groups, these are in group III.

Figure 124

GRAPEVINE AND BRANCHES
Unity of the Church
John 15:5

Jesus said in John 15:5, "I am the vine, you are the branches." Thus a grapevine with branches often symbolizes the unity of the Church. This symbol is in group I.

Figure 125

Figure 126

ANCHOR—Christian Hope
Hebrews 6:19

The *anchor* may have originally been used alone to signify hope, but it seems to have soon picked up the idea of hope of salvation through the cross of Christ (figure 125). The similarity in the shape of an anchor and a cross makes a combination of the two an easy matter (figure 126). This is one of the oldest symbols. Clement of Alexandria, while condemning the too widespread use of symbols, gave his approval to the use of a "ship's anchor" as a Christian seal.

Since there is the specific statement in Hebrews 6:19, "We have this as a sure and steadfast anchor of the soul, a hope that enters into the inner shrine," this symbol should be put either in group I or II, or in both.

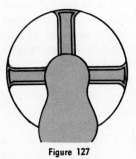

Figure 127

AUREOLE—Divinity
Mark 9:2-13

The *Aureole,* the *Nimbus,* and the *Glory* are man's attempt to picture divinity or divine power. Such an attempt is often known to most of us under the word *halo.* The artist is usually more successful than the writer in picturing that heavenly glow which seems to surround persons who have completely given themselves to God. Both have a difficult time since they are trying to picture or describe a state or quality which in the final analysis comes as a result of the Divine Presence.

67

Figure 128

Figure 129

Early artists attempted to meet this difficulty by standardizing that indescribable glow that seemed to be one manifestation of the Divine Presence. The nimbus surrounds only the head of the person. When the *Nimbus* has the three rays or *Cruciform* in it, as in figure 127, it is used to represent only members of the Trinity. The *Aureole* is an elongated nimbus surrounding the whole body (figure 128). The *Glory* may be best defined as a flood of golden light that proceeds from a group.

Scriptural justification for these attempts to picture the impossible may be found in the story of Moses' return from Mount Sinai, recorded in Exodus 34:29, and the story of the Transfiguration of Jesus, recorded in Mark 9:2-13, Matthew 17:1-13, and Luke 9:28-36.

These symbols of divinity are in group I because even in the scriptures they are symbols of the glow that comes from nearness to God. Their breakdown into specialized categories is, however, not scriptural.

CIRCLE—Eternity

Since a *circle* is without beginning and without end, it is a very appropriate symbol for expressing the eternalness of God. There is no verse of scripture which decrees that a circle should be used to symbolize this great truth about God, but one can easily see that such a symbol is a helpful means of reminding us of God's permanence.

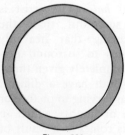

Figure 130

The circle is not usually used alone. It is much more common to see three circles than it is one. The three circles interwoven symbolize the three Persons of the Trinity and their indissoluble union. The circle is also commonly seen combined with the equilateral triangle. (*See* Triangle.)

BAG OF MONEY—Charity
Mark 10:21

Figure 131

If the *money bag* is pictured as being open, it is a symbol of charity to the poor. The appropriateness of this usage may be found in Jesus' command to the rich young ruler, "Go, sell what you have, and give to the poor, and you will have treasure in heaven; and come, follow me." (*See* also Jesus' Betrayal, and Matthew.) This symbol falls into group III.

BIRDS—Human Souls

Figure 132

Many real and imaginary birds have specialized meanings when used as symbols, but the most common explanation for their use in general is that they represent human souls. Even before Christianity the Egyptians pictured souls as having wings. Figure 132, made up of *birds and a Chi Rho,* is from a catacomb carving. Such a symbol is in group III.

For more specialized uses, *see:* Cock, Dove, Eagle, Peacock, Pelican, Phoenix.

GOD'S LOVE

CROSS
Hebrews 12:2

To say that the cross is symbolic of God's love is not to forget the crucifixion of Jesus. It is, rather, to attempt to do in words that which Jesus did by his great example—transform this former symbol of shame, punishment, and death into a symbol of life and love. Even after Jesus' death it was many years before the cross was commonly used as a Christian symbol because of its prior use. Crucifixion or death on a cross was reserved for those persons who in the eyes of their captors were deserving of the most shameful death possible. In Galatians 5:11 Paul speaks of the cross as being a stumbling block. It is probable that Paul's interpretation of Jesus' transfiguration of the cross was the deciding factor in the cross coming to be used as a Christian symbol of God's love.

There are over four hundred kinds of crosses. All of these are not used as Christian symbols, but F. R. Webber in *Church Symbolism* does list more than one hundred and fifty. Many of these are but variations of a basic cross.

Most crosses can be put in one of two groups. Those falling within the group known as *Latin* crosses are distinguished by the fact that the bottom part of the upright piece is longer than either of the arms. Those in the *Greek* group are characterized by arms and upright pieces being of equal length.

LATIN-TYPE CROSSES

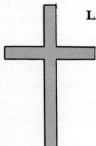

Figure 133

The *Latin Cross* is the most commonly seen cross. It is always shown as being empty, without the body of Christ, in the Evangelical churches because, thus, it represents the risen and living Christ. The crucifix should, therefore, not be used in any church which falls in this category.

Figure 134

The *Graded Cross* is a Latin cross on a base of three steps. These three steps symbolize, beginning with the upper one, faith, hope, and love. This is the usual type of altar cross and is often seen with the monogram *IHC* embossed at the center.

Figure 135

The *Celtic Cross,* sometimes called Ionic or Irish Cross, is so called because an ancient example of this cross is found on the Isle of Iona in western Scotland. This is the place where Irish missionaries began work in Scotland. The circle emphasizes the eternal effect of the redemption secured by the death of Christ on the cross.

Figure 136

The *Budded Cross* received this name because each of its extensions is capped with what appears to be a tree bud (figure 136). Actually these are trefoil designs and are so used to suggest the Trinity. These and almost any of the special designs can be used with the Greek type crosses equally as well as with the Latin type.

71

Figure 137

The *Cross of Victory* is pictured by showing a small Latin cross resting upon a banded globe (figure 137). This symbolizes the triumph of the gospel throughout all the earth. This symbol is particularly appropriate to use in presenting world missions.

For the *Passion Cross* or Cross of Suffering, *see* under chapter IV.

Figure 138

The *Anchor Cross* is a combination of an anchor and a cross (figure 138). Thus it symbolizes salvation through Christ's death and resurrection, and hope in the life eternal. Hebrews 6:19 probably caused this symbol to become popular. Examples of this type of cross are found in the catacombs.

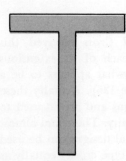

Figure 139

The *Tau Cross* is so named because it resembles the Greek letter of that name. This symbol was used by the Egyptians and others before the time of Christ. The meaning it had for them is obscure. It is also called the Old Testament Cross because, according to tradition, the pole on which Moses lifted up the brazen serpent was a Tau Cross.

GREEK-TYPE CROSSES

The *Greek Cross,* as mentioned before, is formed by using arms and upright members of the same length. It was probably developed by the artistic Greeks as being a more perfect form. This would explain the name.

Figure 140

The *Cross Saltire* or St. Andrew's Cross is, according to tradition, the type of cross on which Andrew was crucified. Tradition says that Andrew was a missionary in Asia Minor and Macedonia, and that he met his death on a cross like this in Greece.

Figure 141

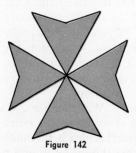

The *Maltese Cross* is formed by four spearheads touching at the center. The eight outer points symbolize the eight Beatitudes. This cross gets its common name from the Island of Malta. A group known as the Knights Hospitalers, that was organized in the eleventh century to protect Christian pilgrims, used this cross as their emblem. The Knights Hospitalers, banished from the Island of Rhodes by the Turks, were permitted to settle on the Island of Malta by Charles V. Thus this cross was called the Maltese Cross.

Figure 142

73

Figure 143

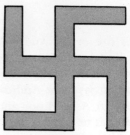

Figure 144

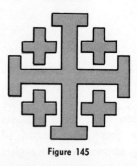

Figure 145

The *Cross Patée,* or **Broad**-footed Cross, is often confused with the Maltese Cross, but they are not the same. The arms of the Cross Patée curve, and the arms of the Maltese Cross are made up of straight lines.

The *Rebated Cross,* Flyfot Cross, or *Crux Grammata* is better known to us by the name of *swastika* (figure 144). It seems to have been connected with sun worship as early as 1500 B.C. But it was used by Christians in the catacombs as symbolic of Christ, "the Sun of Righteousness."

The *Jerusalem Cross,* or Crusader's Cross, is composed of four Tau crosses with their bases joined at the center. Between the arms thus formed are small Greek crosses. This design was first used on the coat-of-arms of the Latin Kingdom of Jerusalem around A.D. 1100. During the Crusades it was used on the shields of the Crusaders. The large center cross is said to symbolize Mosaic Law, and the four smaller Greek crosses symbolize the four Gospels that displaced the Law. It is also used to signify missionary work. In this missionary interpretation, the large cross stands for the original Church in Jerusalem and the smaller crosses remind us of the four corners of the earth to which Christianity has been spread by missions.

The cross is not described in scripture. We, therefore, do not know on which particular type of cross Jesus was crucified. If one agrees that communication of the idea is the more important thing, all of these various types should be in group II. The cross is used in I Corinthians 1:18; Colossians 1:19, 20; and other places as a symbol of Jesus' death and God's love.

Figure 146

CROSS AND CROWN
Death and Heavenly Reward

This symbol is a combination of the *cross* and the *crown*. The cross serves to remind us of Christ's death, and the crown symbolizes the reward of the faithful in life after death. In displaying this symbol, the cross should stand erect rather than at an angle, as it is often seen. This single symbol, formed by a combination of two others, is in group II since one of them is in group I and the other in group II.

Figure 147

Figure 148

HANDS CLASPED
Brotherhood; Marriage

Hands clasped in the form of a handshake are a symbol of Brotherhood. If the hands clasped are those of a man and a woman, they symbolize marriage. Both of these symbols are in group III.

Figure 149

HEART—Christian Love and Service
Matthew 12:34

Since the heart has long been thought to be the center of every impulse to help others, it is a very good symbol of Christian love and the resulting service. This symbol also reminds us of the admonition of Proverbs 4:23, "Keep your heart with all vigilance; for from it flow the springs of life."

The heart as a symbol of Christian love and service is in group II.

75

Figure 150

HEART PIERCED
Luke 2:35

The heart pierced with a sword is the symbol of Mary's suffering as predicted in Luke 2:35. This symbol of the pierced heart is in group II.

Figure 151

PELICAN—The Atonement

Like the peacock, the *pelican* has no specific scriptural origin, but it is a very old and very meaningful Christian symbol of the atoning death of Jesus Christ. The "pelican-in-her-piety" was used in early Christian churches because of the legend that in times of famine the pelican would tear a hole in her breast and feed her young with her own blood, thereby saving them by her own death. Since such a sacrificial love is analogous to that of Christ, this symbol is often used in our churches today to depict his great love and sacrificial death for the world. Since the pelican is not a biblical bird, this symbol falls in group III.

Figure 152

SHIP—The Church

Clement of Alexandria objected to the use of many of the early Christian symbols. But in his own words we have his approval of several symbols. Clement said: "Let our seals be either a dove, or a fish, or a ship scudding before the wind, or a musical lyre, which Polycrates used, or a ship's anchor." In *The Epistle of*

Clement to James, attributed to Clement of Rome, is a statement that helps explain the statement that the ship should be scudding before the wind: "For the whole business of the Church is like unto a great ship, bearing through a violent storm men who are of many places, and who desire to inhabit the city of the good kingdom."

It is interesting to note that the main part of the church is called *nave.* This word comes from the Latin word *navis* which means "ship." Since even this early use is an application not made in scripture, this symbol is in group III. (*See,* also, Apostles, Jude.)

CONCLUSION

A ND the Lord answered me: 'Write the vision; make it plain upon tablets, so he may run who reads it.' " The words Habakkuk wrote changed the life of Paul, of Luther through Paul, and of Wesley through Luther. The message was this: "the righteous shall live by his faith."

We are today faced by the same problems which Habakkuk had to solve—fast living and slow believing. He wrote his message and put it where all might see. So must we. Stained-glass windows, carved doorways, beautiful symbols throughout the church can provide the eye-catching beauty and the soul-stirring inspiration that bring us to our knees. Only there can we receive the faith we need. Then we can run for God.

In symbols we have one of the greatest forces for good that our time will know. They are the signs of the timeless. They weld our efforts with those of the past and link us solidly with the future. In the final analysis all Christians are symbols, symbols of God and his will for man. If our symbols of the Christian faith, those both depicted and lived, were clearer and better known, our plight would be transformed by faith. These are the signposts of timeless devotion. Correctly followed, they will point toward that complete devotion in which we no longer will, but God wills through us. Such a devotion all of us desire and need. To that end this book has been written. May God bless and use it.

The Upper Room Chapel

CHAPTER VIII

SYMBOLISM IN THE UPPER ROOM CHAPEL

by

J. Manning Potts

THE Upper Room Chapel gives effective expression in symbolism to the world's most widely used devotional guide. That the chapel is effective in its expression of the message of prayer and devotion is indicated by the testimonies of thousands who have visited it. It has already proved to be the high point of many a journey—a living shrine. In the years to come it will continue to attract visitors appreciative of its beauty who will find that in a moment of prayer they catch a new appreciation for the meaning of the upper room in Christian experience.

On the day of Pentecost the Holy Spirit fell upon the disciples in the upper room. The great round-topped Georgian window at the front of the building is the creation of Ralph E. Ohmer of the D'Ascenzo Studios, Inc. It is of stained glass and is built around the symbolism of Pentecost. (*See* page 93 for picture of the window.) The other upper room experience memorable to all Christians was the Last Supper.

As one enters the chapel, his attention is focused on the polychrome wood carving of *The Last Supper,* said to be the largest in the world. It is a copy of Leonardo da Vinci's painting and is done in lime wood and walnut. The sculptor was Ernest Pellegrini of the firm of Irving and Casson—A. H. Davenport, Boston and New York. He was a noted Italian sculptor, and his wood carvings are in many of the most noted cathedrals and churches in America. He died in 1955.

The wood carving is an extraordinary work of art. More than fifty workers had a part in completing it. Fourteen months were required for the modeling, carving, and production. As one stands in the doorway and looks at it, he is instantly struck

79

with the perspective of the room in the wood carving; the depth of it is amazing. However, the eye goes immediately to the face of the Christ. It has been said that Leonardo da Vinci painted in his original the saddest face in all the world. Ernest Pellegrini has captured this mood of Christ at the moment when Jesus is saying to his disiciples, "One of you shall betray me."

Each of the twelve disciples is a work of art in itself. From left to right the figures are: Bartholomew, James the Less, Andrew, Peter, Judas, John, Jesus, James the Greater, Thomas, Philip, Matthew, Thaddaeus, and Simon Zelotes. As one stands and looks at the wood carving, he gradually realizes that the chancel and the picture go together. The ceiling in the chancel is like that in the picture. The tapestries on the walls, four on each side, are like the tapestries in the wood carving. The floor is like the floor in Leonardo's painting. The table which serves as the altar is a reproduction of the table in the wood carving. The chancel itself is a reproduction of the room in which Leonardo conceived the Last Supper to have been held.

The next thing which comes into perspective is the chancel rail. One is struck with the symbolism that has been carved upon the shields which rest between the posts of the chancel rail, also the symbolism which is on the gate. Each one of the shields represents an apostle.

Figure 153

PETER

The first is Peter. This shield has an inverted cross with keys. The keys represent Peter's confession, and the cross signifies that Peter at his own request was crucified head downward.

Figure 154

ANDREW

The second is that of Andrew. He is generally represented by an X-like cross. Andrew is supposed to have died in Greece on a cross of this kind.

Figure 155

JAMES THE GREATER

The third shield shows the symbolism of James the Greater. On it are three scallop shells. These signify his pilgrimage and missionary journeys.

Figure 156

JOHN

The fourth shield, with a chalice and a serpent carved upon it, is that of John. This symbolizes the story of an attempt to kill him by poisoning. Legend has it that the priest of Diana gave him poisoned wine to drink. However, he is supposed to have made the sign of the cross over the chalice, and the poison escaped in the form of a serpent.

81

PHILIP

Figure 157

The fifth shield is that of Philip. This shield contains a central cross and two shocks of wheat. The wheat refers to the time when Jesus fed the five thousand and Philip spoke of the bread.

BARTHOLOMEW

Figure 158

The sixth shield is that of Bartholomew. Some believe this to be the same as Nathanael. The shield contains an open Bible. The open Bible represents his preaching of the Word.

THOMAS

Figure 159

The seventh shield, that of Thomas, shows a vertical spear and a carpenter's square. The legend is that Thomas went to East India and erected a church. It is said that he was shot with arrows and that a pagan priest put him to death with a spear.

MATTHEW

Figure 160

The eighth shield is that of Matthew. It has three purses which refer to his early occupation as taxgatherer.

This shield represents Matthew as an apostle. (For Matthew as an evangelist, *see* The Chancel Gate, pages 86, 87.)

JAMES THE LESS

Figure 161

The ninth shield represents James the Less. It has a saw placed vertically with the handle above. There is a legend to the effect that in the ninety-sixth year of his life he was thrown from the top of the Temple and his body sawn asunder. (*See* James the Less, page 55.)

JUDE

Figure 162

The tenth shield shows a sailing ship. It symbolizes the missionary journeys of Jude, who is also known as Thaddaeus or Lebbaeus. He is supposed to have gone to Syria, Arabia, and into Mesopotamia.

83

SIMON ZELOTES

The eleventh shield, that of Simon Zelotes, shows a fish lying on a book. The fish signifies that he was a fisher of men. The book signifies the gospel.

Figure 163

PAUL

The twelfth shield is that of Paul. It contains a rayed cross and represents the spread of the gospel to the world by Paul's missionary journeys and preaching.

Figure 164

THE CHANCEL GATE

On the gate of the chancel one sees the symbolism of the Trinity. The Father is represented by the hand. This is called the *Manus Dei* (hand of God). The hand shows the thumb and the first two fingers extended in the position of blessing, with the third and fourth fingers closed within the palm of the hand. The second figure is the Lamb of God. This is called the *Agnus Dei* with Banner, or the Lamb of God with Banner. The third figure is the Descending Dove, representing the Holy Spirit. The figures on the corners of the gate represent the four Evangelists, with Matthew in the upper left-hand corner, Mark in the upper right-hand corner, Luke in the lower left-hand corner, and John in the lower right-hand corner. (Symbols of four Evangelists are explained on pages 50, 51.)

The models for these wood carvings were made by Professor Puryear Mims, lecturer at Vanderbilt University, and the carving was done by H. J. Kleiser of Nashville, Tennessee.

The Table which serves as the altar is unique not only be-

THE CHANCEL GATE

cause it is a reproduction of the table in the wood carving but also because of its dual purpose: it serves both as the altar and, at times, as Communion table also. The tablecloth used regularly as a centerpiece for the table is dark green plush velvet with a gold fringe.

The symbolism on the cover is a cluster of grapes, representing the Sacrament. The grapes are flanked by the Alpha with cross on the left, and the Omega with cross on the right.

The three altar pieces are antiques. The two silver candlesticks, each twenty-seven inches high, were originally in the private chapel of the Duke of Portsmouth, in England. They date back to about 1700. The chalice is a Persian antique. The Persian Christian tradition is very old. A special feature of the chalice is its delicate etchings. The collar adds to its beauty. It is a very unique piece.

Figure 165

THE CHI RHO ON PULPIT

The high pulpit, with its winding stair; and the canopy, hanging by a gold-leaf chain from the ceiling, are most impressive. The pulpit has features of several very old pulpits; that in the City Road Church, in London, made famous by John Wesley; the St. George's Church, in Philadelphia; and the St. Philip's Church, in Charleston, South Carolina, where Wesley preached on occasion when he was a missionary in Georgia. The pulpit is significant because of its carving.

The symbolism on the front of it is the *Chi Rho,* representing Christ. It is said to be the oldest monogram of the Christ. Sometimes it is called the Christogram. It comes from the Greek spelling of the word *Christ, XPICTOC.*

The marker for the Bible has upon it a sheaf of wheat to represent the bread of life. This is a favorite symbol of the Holy Communion. The sheaf of wheat on the Bible marker and the cluster of grapes on the altar piece represent the Sacrament of the Lord's Supper.

The chapel floor is green and brick-color slate with plastic tile under the pews. The pews are built on the lines of the early Colonial pews with boxed panel ends. The walnut has been carefully selected for its beautiful grain. The color of the wall is ashes of roses. The ceiling is a segment arch with acoustical plaster and has a molded cornice. The ceiling is tinted with green. The wood with which the chapel is paneled throughout is light walnut. The tall, round-arched Georgian windows have cathedral glass with soft green velvet draperies. The pews and the kneeling cushions are dark green plush velvet. Following the practice of early American Colonial churches, the choir is in the loft at the back. The chandeliers are reproductions on a smaller scale of some of the earlier Colonial chandeliers, notably those in St. Michael's Church, Charleston, South Carolina.

THE GROVER C. EMMONS PRAYER ROOM

THE GROVER C. EMMONS PRAYER ROOM

At the left-hand side of the pulpit one enters the small prayer room. It is dedicated to the memory of Grover C. Emmons, who founded *The Upper Room*. The theme of the prayer room is "Alone with God," taken from the title of the little book of prayers by Grover C. Emmons. This prayer room seats only eight people. On the chancel rail one notices the *IHC*. This is said to be the oldest sign for the word *Jesus* in Greek, *IHCOYC*. The two candlesticks are antique baroque Renaissance pieces with cherub and lion symbols. They came from England. The centerpiece is an antique chalice, called a ciborium, a chalice with a cover. Upon it much symbolism is embossed: Jesus washing the feet of the disciples, Jesus in the Garden of Gethsemane, and Jesus on the way to the cross. There one finds also the grapes, the crown of thorns with the three nails, the ladder, reed, and sponge, symbols pertaining to the Crucifixion. At the top of the altar woodwork, the double triangles with the enclosed crosses represent the Trinity and the Crucifixion. The symbols on the altar are the anchor, representing Christian hope; the chalice and cross, representing Gethsemane; and the cross crosslet, representing World Evangelism and the other language editions of *The Upper Room*. Above the altar is a reproduction of the cherubs from the "Sistine Madonna" by Raphael. This painting was done by Professor Gonippi Raggi of Boston, an Italian artist.

Figure 166

CELTIC CROSS OVER CHAPEL

On the capstones over The Upper Room Chapel is a Celtic Cross. Because of an ancient example of this cross that is found on the Isle of Iona in western Scotland, it is sometimes called the Cross of Iona or Ionic Cross. It is made up of a Latin cross and a circle. The cross symbolizes the love of God as revealed by Christ on the cross, and the circle suggests the endless nature of this love. No more appropriate Christian symbol could be found to tower over The Upper Room Chapel and over the home of *The Upper Room*.

THE PENTECOST OR WORLD CHRISTIAN
FELLOWSHIP WINDOW

SYMBOLISM IN THE PENTECOST OR WORLD CHRISTIAN FELLOWSHIP WINDOW

For several years the unique wood carving of *The Last Supper* has been making its appeal to the eyes, minds, and hearts of thousands. They have been persons of all races, of many nations, and of various religious affiliations. Until now the chapel has memorialized only the Last Supper, with Pellegrini's notable wood carving.

On Pentecost Sunday, May 17, 1959, the magnificent, stained-glass window commemorating the coming of the Holy Spirit upon the disciples in the upper room was dedicated. It also depicts other events of that day, both inside and outside the upper room. It interprets the story of Pentecost and the work of the Holy Spirit on that day and through the centuries in the lives of individual heroes of the faith.

The Pentecost Window, twenty feet high and eight feet wide, is the masterful work of the D'Ascenzo Studios, Philadelphia; Ralph Ohmer, President. They have long been known for their fine artistic creations. Their windows adorn many of the great cathedrals and churches of America.

The four large medallions in the window represent events of Pentecost. The first is the gathering of the disciples in the upper room when the Holy Spirit came upon them. The Holy Spirit is represented by tongues of fire. The disciples were filled with the Holy Spirit and spoke as the Spirit gave them utterance. On either side of this medallion are three disciples: one group at prayer, the other selecting Matthias to succeed Judas.

The second of the large medallions represents Peter on the day of Pentecost. The story of his sermon is told in the accompanying smaller medallions. At the top of the second medallion is Joel and at the bottom David. In his sermon, Peter used the words of these two prophets. The smaller medallion to the left depicts the crucifixion, with Mary and John at the cross. The picture at the top and to the right of the medallion of Peter preaching depicts the resurrection morn, with Jesus appearing to Mary Magdalene.

On both sides of the small medallion of David some persons

present on the day of Pentecost are shown. They represent the people from various nations who heard the apostles speak in tongues. Peter preached to those people. The results of his sermon were that they who gladly received his word repented and were baptized.

The third large medallion is a picture of Peter and John at the Beautiful Gate. They received power to heal, and the lame man was enabled to walk. The disciples were brought to trial and put in prison.

Because some of the events of Pentecost happened in the upper room, the supposed building is represented by a medallion, below the picture of Peter and John with the lame man. The symbol for Jesus is on the building. The medallion on one side of the picture represents the love feast, and the medallion on the other side shows some disciples at prayer.

The fourth of the large medallions represents the disciples as they went forth to witness. They became witnesses of the Holy Spirit.

Just below this medallion are two smaller ones, one representing Saul on the road to Damascus and the other representing Stephen, the first Christian martyr.

On the outside border of the Pentecost Window are shown, at the very top, the trefoil and the triangle, symbols of the Trinity: and beneath these is the dove, symbolizing the Holy Spirit. Represented on the left side of the trefoil is Barnabas and, on the right side, St. Augustine. Below Barnabas is St. Bernard of Clairvaux, and below St. Augustine is St. Francis of Assisi.

Other figures represented in the window are George Fox, the Quaker; Martin Luther, father of the Reformation; Isaac Watts and Charles Wesley, hymn writers; John Bunyan, Roger Williams, and Samuel Davies, champions of religious liberty; John Wesley, Jonathan Edwards, George Whitefield, Phillips Brooks, and Alexander Campbell, great preachers; Francis Asbury and William McKendree, pioneer bishops; and also Florence Nightingale and George Washington Carver upon whom the Spirit of God descended in nursing and science.

The small center medallion at the bottom shows John R.

91

Mott, the devoted layman and father of so many Christian youth movements. He is shown here with four representatives from the Far East at the Madras Conference in 1938. That was a great milepost on the road to world Christian fellowship.

The following symbols of the Christian Church are in the window: The trefoil and triangle; dove; lamp; cross of victory; Greek cross; graded cross; chalice and cross; St. Andrew's cross; Tau cross; Noah's Ark, meaning the Church; ship with full sail also symbolizing the Church; the IHC representing Jesus and the Chi Rho for Christ; the vines and grapes; the Bible represented by a book; the bee; the eight-pointed star; the Alpha and Omega; and the symbol which means Jesus Christ the Victor (*see* figure 168).

The window has a complete set of symbols for the apostles, with one for Matthias in place of Judas Iscariot. Symbols representing the apostles are as follows: The cock represents Peter; the scroll, John; basket with Tau cross, Philip; leathern girdle with three stones, Thomas; iron-bound money chest, Matthew; fish impaled on boat hook, Simon Zelotes; pilgrim's staff with wallet on it, James the Greater; x-like cross and great boat hook, Andrew; windmill, James the Less; human skin stretched on a cross, Bartholomew; carpenter's square and boat hook, Thaddaeus or Jude; and a halberd on top of the Bible, Matthias.

Most of the symbols in the window were included in the first edition of this book. The eight symbols given on the following pages are not found elsewhere in this book. Mr. Ratha McGee helped with the material on these symbols.

THE ROSE

The rose is often used in Christian art; and it usually appears in a conventionalized form, as in figure 167. The rose symbolizes the messianic promise. The prophet foretold, "The desert shall rejoice, and blossom as the rose" (Isaiah 35:1. KJ.).

Figure 167

Figure 168

JESUS CHRIST THE VICTOR

This symbol, figure 168, is composed of three Greek words. The two above the arms of the cross are abbreviations. The *IC* represents the Greek word for *Jesus,* which written in capitals is *IHCOYC.* The *XC* represents the Greek word for Christ, which in capitals is *XPICTOC.* The two abbreviations above the arms of the cross mean Jesus Christ. Below the arms of the cross is the Greek word *NIKA,* which means victory. This symbol is usually called Jesus Christ the Victor.

Figure 169

EIGHT-POINTED STAR
Regeneration

The eight-pointed star, figure 169, is the star of baptism or star of regeneration. Eight is symbolically used to mean regeneration. Baptismal fonts are commonly eight sided so that they may symbolize even by their shape the regeneration for which the rite stands. Some say that the number eight came to be used to symbolize rebirth because of the eight souls who were saved from the flood.

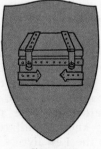

Figure 170

IRON-BOUND MONEY CHEST
Matthew

The Apostle Matthew is sometimes symbolized by an iron-bound money chest, figure 170. Jesus called Matthew from the receipt of custom or tax collecting to follow him. The iron-bound money chest symbolizes that which Matthew willingly gave up to become a disciple of Jesus.

93

Figure 171

CROSS SALTIRE AND GREAT BOAT HOOK
Andrew

The cross saltire with a great boat hook superimposed upon it, figure 171, is used to symbolize Andrew. According to tradition, Andrew died in Greece on a cross like this. The great boat hook symbolizes his original occupation and also the new one. Jesus called him from fisherman to a fisher of men.

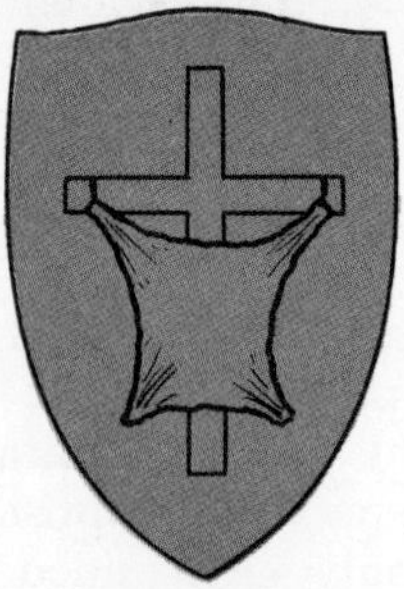

Figure 172

HUMAN SKIN AND CROSS
Bartholomew

Figure 172 reminds us of the cruel death which many of the apostles suffered. This shield of Bartholomew, thought to be the same as Nathanael, shows a cross with a human skin stretched across it. According to one legend, Bartholomew was flayed alive and crucified because of his missionary work.

Figure 173

WINDMILL
James the Less

The windmill on a shield, figure 173, is used to represent the apostle James the Less. The origin of the use of this symbol is unknown. It came into use rather late, for the windmill was not known until centuries after James the Less lived.

94

Figure 174

BOOK AND HALBERD
Matthias

The apostle chosen to replace Judas, Matthias, is depicted by a book and a halberd. This symbol, figure 174, reminds us of his preaching the gospel and of the tradition that he was stoned to death and then beheaded because of his missionary work in Judea.

The window tells the story of Pentecost and the work of the Holy Spirit from the day of Pentecost to modern times. Thus it is a meaningful window, one that will for years to come inspire and challenge many to rededicate themselves to Christ and go forth to increase and strengthen the bonds of faith in world Christian fellowship.

CHAPTER IX

PELLEGRINI'S WOOD CARVING

of

THE LAST SUPPER

Interpreted by

Mildred Anderson Cate

UPON entering The Upper Room Chapel, one's eyes are drawn to the wood carving of *The Last Supper,* made by Ernest Pellegrini. The original painting of *The Last Supper* by Leonardo da Vinci is on the wall of a monastery in Milan, Italy.

In his painting, Leonardo da Vinci wanted everyone to look on Christ first. He used several skillful, artistic ways to get this result. First, he put Christ right in the center. Then he placed the window behind him so the light would outline his head. Notice the arch over that window. Notice also if the lines above the tapestry and the lines of the beamed ceiling were to be continued, they would meet at a place just above Christ's head. This makes Christ the focal point of the scene.

Leonardo da Vinci captured the moment just as Christ said, "One among you shall betray me." Here you see the immediate emotional outbreak caused by that statement. The group of twelve falls into four groups of three each.

At the far left, Bartholomew gets to his feet and leans on the table, staring incredulously at Christ. It seems to me that he is straining to hear every word Christ is saying. He has gotten up in such a hurry that his feet are still crossed. James the Less is trying to get Peter's attention; so he (James the Less) puts his arm around Andrew to touch Peter on the shoulder. James wants Peter to verify the words of Christ.

Andrew throws both hands up, and you can see by the expression on his face the shock and amazement he feels.

In the next group, Peter leans behind Judas to whisper to John. He is probably whispering the words, "Tell us of whom the Master speaks." Judas is leaning on the table, clutching the money bag in his hand. On his face is a look of guilt and fear. John, the beloved disciple, sometimes called the youthful disciple (he was a very young man when Christ called him), closes his eyes in sadness and leans his head toward Peter.

Each one of the group on Christ's left is trying to get his attention. The one sitting next to Christ is James the Greater, one of the sons of Zebedee. Christ called him and his brother John sons of thunder. James throws out both hands and seems to exclaim, "Impossible!" Behind James is Thomas, often described as doubting Thomas. Holding up one finger, he is asking the question, "Lord, is it I?" Of course, that is the question they are all asking, "Is it I?" Philip gets to his feet, and with an expression of love and adoration on his face, wants to bare his heart to Christ to show his innocence.

We see the last group discussing among themselves Christ's shocking statement. Let's skip to the end of the table where Simon Zelotes, or the Zealot, extends both hands and declares his innocence and also his unbelief that any of the disciples would betray the Master. Next to him is Thaddaeus, sometimes called Jude. With an expression of concern and worry, he seems to say, "Surely the Master is mistaken!" Matthew throws out both hands and points to Christ. Looking at the other two in this group, he seems to say, "But he said it is one of us."

Let us look at the face of Christ. The artist has portrayed love, sadness, suffering, and compassion in the Master's face. Our eyes are irresistibly drawn to the eyes of Christ. In one book, Leonardo da Vinci is quoted as saying that he did not feel worthy to paint anything as wonderful as the eyes of Christ. In the carving, as well as the original, the eyes of Christ

98

are cast down; but when you go up to the table and look up into Christ's face, you find that his eyes are open, looking down on you.

To me, there is symbolism in the hands of Christ. The palm of his right hand seems to say, "If possible, let this cup pass from me." The palm of his left hand suggests surrender and resignation, "Nevertheless, not my will, but thine, be done."

But this moment of shock and sadness will soon pass, for Christ will bring comfort and peace to his troubled disciples with the words, "Let not your heart be troubled."

Let's look at the hands of Christ again. The left hand with palm up says to each of us, "Come unto me," while the other with the palm down speaks to us of the outreach of Jesus Christ; it says, "Go and witness for me." Do you see how they balance each other? First, "Come unto me"; then, "Go and witness for me."

GENERAL INDEX

Acrostic, 39

Agnus Dei and Book of Seven Seals, 42, 43; and Banner, 43, 84, 85

Almighty, the, 22

Alpha and Budded Cross, 35, 36

Alpha and Omega, 35, 92

Alpha, Omega and Chi Rho, 35, 36

Alpha, Omega, Cross of Suffering, 36

Alpha, Omega, and Crown, 35, 36

Altar, 65, 66, 84, 85; Burnt Offering, 17

Anchor, 67, 88

Anchor Cross, 67, 72

Andrew, the Apostle, 52, 53, 81, 92, 94, 97

Angelic host, 18

Annunciation, the, 39, 40

Apostles, interpreted, 97-99

Apostles, symbols of,
  Andrew, 52, 53, 81, 92, 94
  Bartholomew, 53, 82, 92, 94
  James the Greater, 54, 81, 92
  James the Less, 55, 83, 92, 94
  John, 55, 81, 91, 92
  Judas Iscariot, 56, 92
  Jude, 57, 83, 92
  Matthew, 57, 58, 83, 92, 93
  Matthias, 58, 59, 92, 95
  Paul, 63, 64, 84
  Peter, 59, 60, 80, 92
  Philip, 60, 61, 82, 92
  Simon Zelotes, 62, 84, 92
  Thomas, 62, 63, 82, 92

Apple, 14, 15

Ark, 15; Covenant, 15, 16; Noah's, 15, 16, 92

Arrows, four, 63

Asbury, Francis, 91

Atonement, 76

Augustine, 91

Aureole, 67, 68

Babel, Tower of, 18

Bag of money, 31, 69

Balances, 19

Banner, 19, 20; Agnus Dei and, 43, 84, 85

Baptism, 27, 54, 93

Barnabas, 91

Bartholomew, the Apostle, 53, 82, 92, 94, 97

Basket, Tau cross, 61, 92

Bat, fuller's, 55

Battle-ax, 58, 59; double, 58

Bee, 92

Bernard of Clairvaux, 91

Betrayal, Christ's, 31, 32

Bible, 49, 50; open, 49, 50, 53, 58, 63, 82, 92

Birds, 69; and a Chi Rho, 69

Boat hook, 57, 62, 92; great, 92, 94

Book and halbert, 92, 95

Book, the, 49, 50, 62, 95

Book of the Seven Seals, 42, 43

Bread of life, 66

Bronze serpent, 29, 30

Brooks, Phillips, 91

Brotherhood, 75

Budded Cross, Alpha and, 35, 36

Bunyan, John, 91

Butterfly, 40, 41

Camel's hair tunic, 51

Campbell, Alexander, 91

Candle, 34, 35

Carpenter's square, 57, 62, 63, 82, 92

Carver, George Washington, 91

Catacomb carving, 69

Celtic Cross over chapel, 88

Censer, 18

Chalice, wafer, Crux Acuta, 30; and snake, 55, 81; and cross, 88, 92

Chancel Gate, the, 84, 85

Chancel rail, 80, 88

Chapel, The Upper Room, 4, 52, 61, 78-99

Charity, 69

Cherubim, 18, 19

101

SYMBOL INDEX
Chronologically Arranged

122. Grapes with sheaves of wheat
123. Sheaves of wheat
124. Grapevine and branches
125. Anchor
126. Anchor Cross
127. *Cruciform Nimbus*
128. Aureole
129. Glory
130. Circle
131. Bag of money
132. Birds and Chi Rho
133. Latin Cross
134. Graded Cross
135. Celtic Cross
136. Budded Cross
137. Cross of Victory
138. Anchor Cross
139. Tau Cross
140. Greek Cross
141. Cross Saltire

142. Maltese Cross
143. Cross Patée
144. Rebated Cross
145. Jerusalem Cross
146. Cross and crown
147. Clasped hands (Brotherhood)
148. Clasped hands (Marriage)
149. Heart
150. Pierced heart
151. Pelican
152. Ship
153. Inverted Cross and keys
154. Cross Saltire
155. Three scallop shells
156. Chalice with snake
157. Cross and shocks of wheat
158. The open Bible

159. Vertical spear and carpenter's square
160. Three money bags
161. Vertical handsaw
162. Ship at full sail
163. Book with fish
164. Rayed Cross
165. Chi Rho
166. Celtic Cross
167. The rose
168. Jesus Christ the Victor
169. Eight-pointed star, regeneration
170. Iron-bound money chest
171. Cross Saltire and great boat hook
172. Human skin on Cross
173. Windmill
174. Book and halberd